ALL THE SAINTS ADORE THEE

Insight From Christian Classics

BRUCE SHELLEY

Zondervan Publishing House
Grand Rapids, Michigan

All the Saints Adore Thee
Copyright © 1988 by Bruce L. Shelley

Daybreak Books are published by the Zondervan Publishing House
1415 Lake Drive, S.E., Grand Rapids, Michigan 49506

Library of Congress Cataloging-in-Publication Data

All the saints adore thee : insights from Christian classics / [compiled] by Bruce L. Shelley.
    p. cm.
  ISBN 0-310-51501-7
  1. Spiritual life. I. Shelley, Bruce L. (Bruce Leon), 1927–.
  BV4501.2.A378   1988
  248–dc 19   88–14913
                                                         CIP

Edited by Nia Jones

Designed by Martha Manikas-Foster

Printed in the United States of America

88 89 90 91 92 93 / CH / 10 9 8 7 6 5 4 3 2 1

Contents

Part 5: Saints in the Age of Revivals 125

Part 6: Saints in Modern Times 181

Preface

As I recall, it was Soren Kierkegaard, the melancholy Dane, who wrote in his *Journals,*"God creates out of *nothing*. Wonderful, you say. Yes, to be sure, but he does what is still more wonderful: He makes saints out of sinners."

This little volume is concerned with the ways God does that. It grew up in my classroom. For years and years I have been teaching church history in an evangelical seminary. At the beginning of most class hours I have tried to introduce a hymn, a quotation, or an anecdote from the slice of history before us that day. These had to be small but, like the rabbit in the dog race, they had to set the pace for the whole hour. That is how I turned to brief words of counsel from the saints of the past.

While teaching another course, an elective called "Christian Spiritual Classics," I discovered how miserably little today's candidates for Christian ministry knew about the saints. I assigned each student two full-length devotional classics, but I often found that today's student had practically no background from which to make an intelligent choice. He or she had trouble distinguishing flowers from weeds. That is when I decided that a bouquet might be a good idea, a few flowers from many sources.

For both of these reasons, then, this anthology has a wide variety of brief readings, long enough to open a class or introduce a student to a saint. I have the additional hope that these short selections will encourage other believers beyond the classroom to draw nearer to God in their personal devotional times, by meeting some very special "friends of God" from the past.

The idea for 52 chapters came to me while reading Richard Baxter's *The Saints' Everlasting Rest*. He says at one point that the Lord's Day is "exceeding seasonable" for meditation. "When should we more seasonably contemplate our rest than on that day of rest which typifies it to us?" So the overall design of the book reflects our hope that some Christians will want to use its pages as a weekly stimulus to meditation. I am sure Baxter, as I, would be pleased.

Bruce L. Shelley
Denver Seminary
Summer, 1987

Introduction

Near our home, nestled in the foothills of the Rocky Mountains, lies holy ground for American Catholics. The Mother Cabrini Shrine, just above Golden, Colorado, is dedicated to America's first Roman Catholic saint and patron of emigrants and displaced persons.

Overlooking Denver and Colorado's eastern plains, this hallowed site has all the symbols of other sacred landscapes in Frances Cabrini's native Italy. Hundreds of steps, lined by the stations of the cross, lead to the peak of the ridge where Mother Cabrini drew on the ground her sacred heart of devotion to Jesus. In the chapel, row upon row of burning candles loft the prayers of devout Catholics to the saint, looking down on the scene with otherworldly serenity. And on the very spot where Mother Cabrini smote the rock, like a female Moses, miraculous water offers hope of healing to suffering pilgrims here or dying invalids at home.

"Saints" have always been a part of the Roman Catholic experience. Names of American cities even testify to the contribution the saints have made in taming the continent. Saint Louis, San Diego, Santa Barbara, San Antonio, and San Francisco are the most obvious examples. In the same way, parochial schools, under the protection of some saint, continue to create those shocking headlines in the sports sections of the metropolitan newspapers: "Saint Joseph beats Holy Family." And what driver in urban areas doesn't recall seeing a Saint Christopher on the dashboard of some motorist's car?

Protestant piety seems dull by comparison. Baptists, Presbyterians, Lutherans, and other Protestants somehow must cultivate their love for God without the help of thousands of colorful characters from church history and even folklore.

Protestants have their reasons for rejecting the saints in the traditional Roman Catholic sense. "Saints as miracle-workers and go-betweens," they say, "lead to an erroneous and dangerous conclusion about the Christian faith. We don't really need these saints. Jesus is all we need."

In this book about Christian devotion, perhaps I had better underscore that conviction from the start. No human being, living or dead, should ever supplant the Lord Jesus Christ in the Christian's worship. He didn't leave us that option. "I am the bread of life," he said. And that was only one of hundreds of such claims. He is absolutely unique. Let that be abundantly clear.

Are we to draw from that fact, however, that no place remains in the devotional life for other ordinary Christian believers who have experienced the grace of God in an extraordinary way? Can't we benefit from the counsel of men and women in earlier times who explain to us what it means to live vibrantly for God? Can't we, in fact, see the Lord himself reflected in His servants and understand more readily what God can do with human nature?

9

In his book *The Pure in Heart,* W. E. Sangster, the highly respected English Methodist, pointed out that we grow like the people we admire. If the longing for holiness is to be awakened in us, then we must see, not only its perfection in the Savior, but approximations to it in ordinary Christians made extraordinary by God's power.

The Bible encourages us to ponder the lives of spiritual models. In the eleventh chapter of the Book of Hebrews, for example, we find a "hall of faith" from the Old Testament. "Abel," we read, "offered God a better sacrifice. . . . Abraham, when God tested him, offered Isaac as a sacrifice. . . . Moses, when he had grown up, refused to be known as the son of Pharaoh's daughter." By reviewing the struggles and victories of certain spiritual heroes out of Israel's past, we are encouraged to ponder the lives of other saints.

In this book we meet an array of spiritual guides from Christian history— saints, if you please—who continue that ancient tradition. We have so much to learn from them. In our constantly shifting world, we need their spiritual perspective, their reminders that there is another world that knows neither the clouds of death nor the tears of pain. God is there and it is possible to live our lives here and now in the light of His presence.

We are not only concerned in these pages with something deeper and wider than Christian doctrine. We want to discover the meaning of personal devotion to Christ, and that is something more basic than our thoughts about God. Who can surpass Will Sangster's description of devotion in his *The Pure in Heart?* "Just as man knows the surface of the sea," he wrote, "and perhaps a few hundred feet beneath it, but is aware that the ocean is over six miles deep in places, and that the vast unexplored depths constantly affect the shallow area of his knowledge, so the devout believer knows that beneath the area of ordered thought there is a vast ocean. He cannot speak in clear terms and with detailed understanding about his subterranean world but he feels its pull, and knows its effect, and enjoys experiences from it that he cannot put into plain words."

What a helpful picture! This book contains the testimony and teaching of fifty-two saints, men and women who walked with God and knew how to carry on a conversation with the Almighty. I like to think of them as the heroes and heroines of the Christian faith.

Even in our secular societies, we all have our heroes. We seem to need them and naturally want to look up to those we admire. Hero worship is in our genes. Sometimes our rulers satisfy that longing; sometimes, our athletic giants; sometimes, our movie stars, or entertainment idols. But we all seem to need someone with power, talent, or sanctity greater than our own.

In the church, the term for our heroes is "saints." It is time to define the word "saint." After all, we are not talking about a football team or a dashboard memento.

In the Roman Catholic Church and the Eastern Orthodox Church, a "saint" means one who has been "canonized." In the early churches, canonization meant to place the names of the saints in the Canon of the Mass.

This list of recognized saints was the original way the churches identified their heroes, their spiritual athletes. The passing of the centuries, however, added so many to the exalted roll that it was not possible to mention them all in the Mass.

In time, both Western and Eastern churches created complicated processes to determine and designate their "saints." For nearly a thousand years in the Roman Catholic Church the apparatus for canonization required petitions from the dead candidate's sponsors and well-wishers, a dossier of his good deeds, and a devil's advocate whose function was to pick flaws in the case for the candidate. A saint was one who passed the tests.

This revered status recognized the saint's access to God and made him (or her) a subject for prayers from those on earth. He could intercede with God for struggling Christians below. And he could become a "patron," a kind of advocate with God for sailors, watchmakers, runaways, or any other group in special need.

Eventually a distinctive type of literature called hagiography arose, which described the lives of the saints. The writing tended to be pious and sanctimonious rather than accurate or stirring. Their point was not factual history but personal inspiration. Mindless zeal, however, can generate a frenzy for the miraculous, and that is what happened. The legendary Saint Gothard, for example, is supposed to have hung his cloak on a sunbeam, while Sabrinus, who understood the language of birds, preached to them note by note. These are only typical of many stories, all aimed at the overthrow of our sensibilities.

In the last generation, the Vatican has cast a disapproving glance at some of these excesses. It has declared that two hundred of these saints listed in the calendar of saints are no longer worthy objects of veneration. Some of them may never have existed; others have become so encrusted with outrageous miracles as to become unbelievable. Although most of these dethroned heroes were too obscure to cause any furor in the church, many devout Catholics have resisted the forced retirement of St. Valentine, St. Nicholas, and St. Christopher.

Protestants tend to smile at all of this because they have no official roster of saints, no way to canonize them, and no practice of praying to them. They know that the pages of the New Testament do not use the term in this way.

In the days of the apostles, saint meant a Christian, any Christian. For example, when the apostle Paul writes to the church at Philippi, he greets all the "saints in Christ Jesus" (Philippians 1:1). These are obviously not departed members of the church but living believers. And this text is simply typical of the way saint appears in the New Testament writings.

Protestants have tried to return to this New Testament use of the term. They don't believe that the church has the power to canonize anyone. Only God can make a saint and only God can know when one is made. Which of us, for example, has not been shocked, during some moment of self-examination, to discover an evil deep within our own souls? If men do not know their own hearts, how can they possibly judge the spiritual condition of others? So when a Protestant refers to a saint, he has no miracle worker in mind. He is thinking of a Christian believer he admires for his or her sanctity, which is precisely what I have in mind in this book.

Unfortunately, most Protestants today are all but ignorant of a historic succession of spiritual counselors who can broaden and deepen their devotional lives. This sampler of spiritual counsel from across the Christian centuries is designed to address that need.

The book, however, is no hagiography. I do not intend to sing the praises of the men and women we meet in these pages. Aside from two or three accounts of Christian martyrdom, I have in mind not what they did so much as what they said. While their lives are important evidence of the grace of God, their words point beyond their own experiences to the meaning of genuine devotion. These authors, then, are not so much self-proclaimed models of the Christian life as they are coaches.

There are reasons behind my range of choices. I hope to show that the search for a satisfying walk with God is a timeless quest. Men and women of every age speak of their fellowship with the Almighty. So I have included saints from the days of the apostles, from the twentieth century, and from every age in between.

The saints in this book come from a host of denominational labels: Quakers, Roman Catholics, Lutherans, Baptists, and a string of others. This variety is not intended to discount the importance of theology. Actually I have my own questions about the way some of these believers speak of certain elements of their faith. But I hope to show that in the devotional life, God understands the intentions of the human heart, even when we have trouble expressing the thoughts within our heads.

Readers will also discover that saints come from an assortment of cultures and callings: Jews, North Africans, and Germans; preachers, nuns, and prisoners. Again, Christ is the One for all seasons and all saints.

What, then, are the saints telling us? I have no objection to the term if we understand that Christians have always insisted that the redemptive life of God is possible only through faith in Christ. Unfortunately, contemporary scholars do not always recognize that limitation. Many of them use "spirituality" to include almost any experience with almost any god that anyone can have through almost any religious tradition.

The term "mysticism" poses similar problems. It, too, suffers from overuse. Often it suggests that the spiritual person can be in fundamental accord with God because man and God share some fundamental nature, some basic "spirit" or "soul."

Such an idea is unacceptable to orthodox Christians, who hold that there is something distinctive about Christian "mysticism." They insist that true "mystics" always distinguish God from their own subjectivity. God retains a separate existence apart from their experience of Him. And their encounter with God is never an escape from life. It is always in the midst of life's problems and is always through faith in the Christ who came to Bethlehem and was "crucified under Pontius Pilate."

These difficulties with "spirituality" and "mysticism" have driven me to the old term "devotion." While it has its own weaknesses, not the least of which is its suggestion of emotional attachment, I like the term. It combines two ideas that are essential to the Christian's spiritual life, namely, love for God expressed in worship and allegiance to God expressed by life in the world.

What we hope to study, then, is the devotion to Jesus Christ of those who, over the years have professed to know him in a personal way. The anonymous author of the Book of Hebrews in the New Testament says, "Jesus Christ is the same yesterday and today and forever" (Hebrews 13:8). If that is true, we can hear his voice in the testimony of the saints.

This book is organized in historical sequence to demonstrate the unity of the saints' testimonies, even amid an astonishing diversity in their lives and times. There really is a communion of saints across the centuries. The similarities between the saints' spiritual struggles are striking. Self-will, confession of sin, and freedom through forgiveness are essentially the same, whether in the second century or the twentieth. Since many people have a limited knowledge of Christian history, I have included brief introductions along the way.

Obviously many other saints could have been included in this volume, but I have chosen those who, I feel, seem to speak most directly to contemporary Christians. I can only hope that the saints I have chosen will demonstrate that the grace of God is available in every generation.

Despite the fact that I have searched for the best translations of the original quotations, the writing style is not always contemporary. If a few "thees" and "thous" slow us down a bit, perhaps that is to the good because we should not consume literature of this sort too hastily.

Part 1

Saints in the Early Church

"When The Saints Go Marchin'" is a perennial favorite of marching bands. The rhythm insists that everyone within five blocks join the celebration. Tap those feet! Move on down the road!

Unfortunately, today's crowds along the parade route may not catch the old song's message.

I had a lovin' brother,
Death released him from sin,
And I promised I would meet him,
When the saints go marchin' in.

For years, as I understand it, the melody and the message were played by black musicians for funerals in New Orleans and other Southern cities. That's only fitting. Saints have always had a lot to say about death and about "marchin'" into Glory. This idea is as old as Christianity.

Historians call the early centuries of the Christian church "the age of martyrs" because these were the days when saints loved God and served their neighbors in the shadow of death. Although events determined that this theme was often in the hearts and minds of these saints, death was never their last word. "Marchin'" into Glory was possible, they claimed, because of Jesus Christ.

The founder and Savior of Christianity had died on a Roman cross. So a special death was at the heart of the Christian gospel. Jews and Romans, however, considered crucifixion a repulsive way to launch a religion, and they seized every opportunity to let Christians know how they felt. As a result, Christianity grew from a despised sect within Judaism, to an unlawful "superstition" within the Roman Empire, to the established religion of the Empire by keeping death and its remedy before the minds of people. The antidote, Christians claimed, was Jesus.

THE TIMES

Jesus of Nazareth was a son of Judaism. The backdrop of his life and mission was the saga of Israel in the wilderness, in the Promised Land, and in Gentile captivity. He considered his own mission a continuation of the Lord God's saving plan at work in Abraham, Moses, David, and Jeremiah. The questions he fired at the Jewish leaders of his time were the questions of historic Judaism: What is the purpose of the Law? How does a person walk humbly before his God? What is righteousness? Is there any power stronger than death?

Jesus' conflict with the Jewish authorities came from the fact that his answers to these questions focused sharply upon himself. He was the fulfillment of the Law. He was the Lord's only guide to righteousness. He held the keys to death and hell.

Opposition to Jesus hardened to the point where elimination of the "blasphemer" seemed like the only sensible course of action for the Jewish leaders. So the authorities seized him, delivered him to the Romans, and watched him die on a cross. They assumed that would end the matter, but they were wrong, totally wrong.

Within days Jesus' followers, now outcasts of official Judaism, were claiming to be "the true children of Abraham." Their crucified friend, they announced, was none other than the Messiah, Israel's long-awaited Liberator! God himself had demonstrated the fact by raising him from the dead. That fact—life after death—was the heart of the original devotion to Jesus.

The shift of the Jesus movement from Judaism to the wider Gentile world came through a short, zealous disciple called Paul of Tarsus. Thanks to his remarkable conversion, he saw clearly that Jesus' death was far more than a tragic end to a beautiful life. He found in Jesus' death God's gift of salvation, not simply for the Jews but for all peoples. And he preached this message boldly in synagogues and arenas all over the northern shore of the Mediterranean. In his letters to the churches that sprouted from his tireless travel, Paul spoke of Jesus not merely as a past hero to be remembered and admired but as a living person, unseen but "at hand," who met with his people in corporate worship and in private prayer.

With the growth of the movement in the Greco-Roman world came the threat of suppression by the Romans. This conflict with Rome raged over a fundamental civic issue: To whom do I owe ultimate allegiance? Romans allowed religions within the Empire to believe and teach what they pleased, but one thing they would not tolerate: disloyalty to the empire. "Caesar is Lord," they insisted. But that is just what a Christian would not say.

As long as the Romans considered Christians just another sect of Judaism, they granted them the same special toleration extended to the Jews. But when Roman officials recognized the differences between Jews and Christians, they struck out at the growing "superstition" called Christianity. At first this persecution was limited to local areas, but in the third century, emperors launched systematic, empire-wide purges. Thousands of Christians died.

One of the primary defenses Christians raised against this onslaught was their simple, upright lifestyle. "How," they asked, "can such unassuming, loyal people be subversives? We are no threat to the Emperor; our allegiance is to a Lord who said, 'My kingdom is not of this world.'"

The all-out policy of persecution lasted, on and off, for half a century before the Emperor Constantine (c. 274–337) saw it for what it was, a failure. Constantine was shrewd enough to see that Christian churches had actually multiplied, so he tried the opposite policy. Why not enlist the Christian God for imperial service? And his gamble paid off. After defeating his rival, Maxentius, on the battlefield in A.D. 312, he brought the church under imperial protection, lavished it with favors, and assumed responsibility for its faith and fortunes.

Some Christians welcomed the link between church and state, just as some defend it today. Other Christians were not so sure that state support was a gift from God. In either case, Christians, for the first time, had the leisure to think deeply and devoutly about what it meant to know and love the living God. The six brief chapters that follow illustrate how early saints demonstrated and spoke of their love for Jesus Christ.

Bound to Christ's Love

PAUL OF TARSUS

C omfort must be one of the basic necessities of life. Men and women in our society often work long hours, spend thousands of dollars, and sacrifice family and friends for one primary goal—their personal comfort. Because comfort is so important to us, we are mystified by religious zealots. We can't understand people who are eager to forego personal pleasures to translate the Bible for an isolated tribe of people in Brazil or open a drug treatment center in Harlem.

Devotion, allegiance driven by love, is the key. Devoted people have had someone enter their lives and dethrone personal pleasure in their hearts. In the words of one of Jesus' earliest disciples: "Christ's love compels us." Paul of Tarsus was a little giant in the early church, "little" because he was physically short and unimpressive, but "giant" because no one other than Jesus himself has had such an impact upon Christianity.

Prior to his conversion, Paul was one of the chief persecutors of the Jesus movement. He acquired his education in Jerusalem from one of the leading rabbis of the day, a man named Gamaliel, and assumed leadership in the sect of the Pharisees. He was a champion of the traditional Jewish religion.

But in the midst of his rage against the Christians, he experienced a sudden and dramatic conversion to faith in Jesus. After early years of ministry in Syria and his native Cilicia in Asia Minor, Paul launched into a series of missionary trips that eventually reached the major cities of Greece and probably even Rome itself.

Zealous missionaries, however, have a way of provoking opposition. Paul did, and his own former colleagues in Judaism hounded him to death at the hands of the Roman authorities. He apparently died in the capital of the Empire, in Rome, where he had purposed to go for a number of years.

In his highly influential letter to the church at Rome, he reveals the secret of his changed life and the basis of every Christian believer's devotion: the unsurpassing love of Christ. This love, according to Paul, is more satisfying than personal comfort and stronger than the chains of death.

JUSTIFIED!

We know that in all things God works for the good of those who love him, who have been called according to his purpose. For those God foreknew he also predestined to be conformed to the likeness of his Son, that he might be the firstborn among many brothers. And those he predestined, he also called; those he called, he also justified; those he justified, he also glorified.

What, then, shall we say in response to this? If God is for us, who can be against us? He who did not spare his own Son, but gave him up for us all— how will he not also, along with him, graciously give us all things? Who will bring any charge against those whom God has chosen? It is God who justifies. Who is he that condemns? Christ Jesus, who died—more than that, who was raised to life—is at the right hand of God and is also interceding for us. Who shall separate us from the love of Christ? Shall trouble or hardship or persecution or famine or nakedness or danger or sword? As it is written:

> "For your sake we face death all day long;
> we are considered as sheep to be slaughtered."

No, in all things we are more than conquerors through him who loved us. For I am convinced that neither death nor life, neither angels nor demons, neither the present nor the future, nor any powers, neither height nor depth, nor anything else in all creation, will be able to separate us from the love of God that is in Christ Jesus our Lord.[1]

Christians in the World

THE LETTER TO DIOGNETUS

C hristians in our society often give immense importance to the approval of non-Christians. "What will others think?" is never far from the center of our thoughts. However, with that attitude we must be careful not to make too many compromises with evil.

Jesus warned his disciples that they should expect the world's hostility not praises. "If the world hates you," he said, "keep in mind that it hated me first. . . . If they persecuted me, they will persecute you also. . . . In this world you will have trouble. But take heart! I have overcome the world."

As we have seen, that trouble came first from the Jews, then from the Romans. Stephen, a leader in the church at Jerusalem, was the first Christian martyr. But others soon followed. For almost three centuries, ignorance, suspicion, rumors, and hatred combined to create an oppressive climate for Christians.

Christians often defended themselves with explanations of their beliefs and practices; however, the most telling response was the Christian lifestyle. "How can we be as vile as you charge," Christians asked, "when we live the way we do?" This argument for Christian truth has not often been heard in the church. But in the early days it was effective because pagans could not deny it.

Perhaps the most attractive portrait of early Christians in a hostile world is from the pen of an anonymous believer in the early second century. It is called the *Letter to Diognetus*. From this little letter we can see how early Christians lived in the world without surrendering to its power. Such a description of the Christian life doesn't speak to the question of devotion directly, but it strongly suggests that such a life in the world is impossible apart from constant contact with another "hidden world." We know this author had a special way with words and was familiar with the Gospel of John and the letters of Paul.

And Diognetus? We know little more about him than about the author. He may have tutored the youngster in the Roman imperial court who later became the Stoic philosopher-emperor Marcus Aurelius Antonius (A.D. 121–180).

What we do know is the letter asks Christians then and now, "What about your life? Do people find anything attractive, different in it?"

CITIZENSHIP

Christians cannot be distinguished from the rest of the human race by country or language or customs. They do not live in cities of their own; they do not use a peculiar form of speech; they do not follow an eccentric manner of life. This doctrine of theirs has not been discovered by the ingenuity or deep thought of inquisitive men, nor do they put forward a merely human teaching, as some people do.

Yet though they live in Greek and barbarian cities alike, as each man's lot has been cast, and follow the customs of the country in clothing and food and other matters of daily living, at the same time they give proof of the remarkable and admittedly extraordinary constitution of their own commonwealth.

They live in their own countries, but only as aliens. They have a share in everything as citizens, and endure everything as foreigners. Every foreign land is their fatherland, and yet for them every fatherland is a foreign land. They marry, like everyone else, and they beget children, but they do not cast out their offspring. They share their board with each other, but not their marriage bed.

It is true that they are "in the flesh," but they do not live "according to the flesh." They busy themselves on earth, but their citizenship is in heaven. They obey the established laws, but in their own lives they go far beyond what the laws require.

They love all men, and by all men are persecuted. They are unknown, and still they are condemned; they are put to death, and yet they are brought to life. They are poor, and yet they make many rich; they are completely destitute, and yet they enjoy complete abundance. They are dishonored, and in their dishonor are glorified; they are defamed, and are vindicated. They are reviled, and yet they bless; when they are affronted, they still pay due respect. When they do good, they are punished as evil doers; undergoing punishment, they rejoice because they are brought to life. They are treated by the Jews as foreigners and enemies, and are hunted down by the Greeks and all the time those who hate them find it impossible to justify their enmity.

To put it simply: what the soul is in the body, that Christians are in the world. The soul is dispersed through all the members of the body, and Christians are scattered through all the cities of the world. The soul dwells in the body but does not belong to the body, and Christians dwell in the world, but do not belong to the world.[2]

3

Faithful Unto Death

THE MARTYRDOM OF POLYCARP (c. 155)

C hristian martyrs have always fascinated surviving believers. They still do. Think of the popularity of *Foxe's Book of Martyrs* over the years. Or of the magnetism of Dietrich Bonhoeffer's suffering from our twentieth-century perspective. What is it like to face the ultimate choice: Christ or death? Is God unusually real to a believer about to pass over to the other side?

In the early years of the church (A.D. 30–312), when martyrdoms at the hands of Roman officials were common, such questions led first to the admiration of martyrs, then to their veneration in Christian worship. History transformed Christian martyrs into Catholic saints.

We need not go as far as the Church of Rome did during the Middle Ages to admire the steadfast faith and supernatural courage of the martyrs. The Epistle to the Hebrews calls us to greater faith by reminding us of ancient believers who were faithful even in death.

The martyrdom of Polycarp is one of the better-known stories from the pages of early Christian history. We have no idea who the original author was, but we know Polycarp himself rather well. He was apparently a disciple of the apostle John who served as bishop (or pastor) of the Church at Smyrna, not far from Ephesus. We have a letter he wrote to the Philippian church, but over the years Christians have remembered him most often as the steadfast martyr who dared to defy the Roman authorities in the year 155 or 156.

When riots against Christians first broke out in Smyrna, Polycarp's friends urged him to withdraw to a farm outside the city. He did. But when members of his own household disclosed his hideout, police came to arrest him and delivered him to the proconsul at the city arena, which was crowded with spectators awaiting the execution of the notorious leader of the Christians.

AN ACCEPTABLE SACRIFICE

And when finally he [Polycarp] was brought up, there was a great tumult on hearing that Polycarp had been arrested. Therefore, when he was brought before him, the proconsul asked him if he were Polycarp. And when he confessed that he was, he tried to persuade him to deny [the faith], saying, "Have respect to your age"—and other things that customarily follow this, such as, "Swear by the fortune of Caesar; change your mind; say, 'Away with the atheists!' "

But Polycarp looked with earnest face at the whole crowd of lawless heathen in the arena, and motioned to them with his hand. Then groaning and looking up to heaven, he said, "Away with the atheists!"

But the proconsul was insistent and said: "Take the oath, and I shall release you. Curse Christ."

Polycarp said: "Eighty-six years I have served him, and he never did me any wrong. How can I blaspheme my King who saved me?"

The proconsul said, "Try to persuade the people."

But Polycarp said, "You, I should deem worthy of an account; for we have been taught to render honor, as is fitting, to rulers and authorities appointed by God so far as it does us no harm; but as for these, I do not consider them worthy that I should make a defense to them."

And when he had said these things and many besides he was inspired with courage and joy, and his face was full of grace, so that not only did it not fall with dismay at the things said to him, but on the contrary, the proconsul was astonished, and sent his own herald into the midst of the arena to proclaim three times: "Polycarp has confessed himself to be a Christian."

When this was said by the herald, the entire crowd of heathen and Jews who lived in Smyrna shouted with uncontrollable anger and a great cry: "This one is the teacher of Asia, the father of the Christians, the destroyer of our gods, who teaches many not to sacrifice nor to worship."

Then these things happened with such dispatch, quicker than can be told—the crowds in so great a hurry to gather wood and faggots from the workshops and the baths, the Jews being especially zealous, as usual, to assist with this. . . .

And with his hands put behind him and tied, like a noble ram out of the great flock ready for sacrifice, a burnt offering ready and acceptable to God, he looked up to heaven and said:

"Lord God Almighty, Father of the beloved and blessed Servant Jesus Christ, . . . I bless thee, because thou hast deemed me worthy of this day and hour, to take part in the number of martyrs, in the cup of thy Christ, for 'resurrection to eternal life' of the soul and body in the immortality of the Holy Spirit; among whom may I be received in thy presence this day as a rich and acceptable sacrifice, just as thou has prepared and revealed beforehand and fulfilled, thou that art the true God without falsehood. For this and everything I praise thee, I bless thee, I glorify thee, through the eternal and heavenly

High Priest, Jesus Christ, thy beloved Servant, through whom be glory to thee with him and the Holy Spirit both now and unto the ages to come. Amen.''

And when he had concluded the Amen and finished his prayer, the men attending to the fire lighted it. . . .

So we later took up his bones, more precious than costly stones and more valuable than gold, and laid them away in a suitable place.[3]

A Christian View of Death

4

THASCIUS CYPRIAN (c. 200–258)

A generation or two ago people often recorded and remembered the last words of important people or loved ones. This custom has almost vanished, perhaps in large part since most people die today quietly in some hospital room or rest home—alone. Maybe this isn't good. Last words to or from a dying soul can be inspiring expressions of faith and courage.

John Wesley's last words are a challenge to this day. "The best of all," he said, "God is with us." And I have always appreciated that beautiful last sentence from Peter Marshall, the Chaplain of the United States Senate. In his biography, *A Man Called Peter,* his wife tells how, as he was being carried from his house on a stretcher on his way to the hospital, he said to her, "I'll see you in the morning." That night he died. But the words are a beautiful expression of the Christian faith in the hour of our greatest crisis.

In the early days of the church, Christians confronted death almost daily. It could come before nightfall. In such an atmosphere, spiritual guides had to know how to face reality and what to say. Thascius Cyprian was apparently such a guide.

Cyprian found no preparation for the Christian faith in his home. He came from a wealthy and highly cultivated, but pagan, family. He probably grew up in Carthage, near today's Tunis in North Africa.

Then, during his adult years, he made a fateful decision. He professed personal faith in Jesus Christ as Savior, just when it was becoming unhealthy to own the name. He was baptized, probably in the year 246, and moved quickly, by popular demand, into positions of Christian leadership at Carthage. By the beginning of 249, he was bishop of the city, an office of considerable influence in the early church, and a position of danger.

Later that year, a traditionally-minded Roman emperor named Decius launched the first empire-wide persecution of the Christians. Death became a common experience in Christian households. Many Christians at Carthage denied the faith rather than suffer the ultimate price for taking Christ's name. Cyprian himself survived temporarily because he fled the city to preserve leadership in the church.

In 251, when Emperor Decius was killed on the battlefield, the persecution fell into a temporary lull. In 257, however, under the Emperor Valerian, persecution broke out afresh. This time Cyprian himself was seized and confined. From his captivity he tried to bring comfort to his colleagues, nine of whom were languishing in the mines at Sigua, not far away. The letter he wrote to them is perhaps his most eloquent appeal for faith in the face of suffering and death. On September 14, 258, not far from Carthage, Cyprian followed his colleagues in death. He was beheaded.

Here is his letter to his friends in the mines.

ORNAMENTS OF CHAINS

Cyprian to . . . Felix, Victor, Jader, . . . and the rest of the brethren in the mines, martyrs of God the Father Almighty, and of Jesus Christ our Lord, and of God our preserver, everlasting greeting.

Your glory, indeed, would demand, most blessed and beloved brethren, that I myself should come to see and to embrace you, if the limits of the place appointed me did not restrain me, banished as I am for the sake of the confession of the Name. But what way I can, I bring myself into your presence, . . . in love and in spirit I come expressing my mind in my letter. . . .

Could I be silent and restrain my voice in stillness, when I am made aware of so many and such glorious things concerning my dearest friends. . . ? As golden and silver vessels, you have been committed to the mine that is the home of gold and silver, except that now the nature of the mines is changed, and the places which previously had been accustomed to yield gold and silver have begun to receive them.

Moreover they have put fetters on your feet, and have bound your blessed limbs, and the temples of God with disgraceful chains, as if the spirit could be stained by the contact with iron. To men who are dedicated to God, and attesting their faith with religious courage, such things are ornaments, not chains; nor do they bind the feet of the Christians for infamy, but glorify them for a crown. Oh feet blessedly bound, which are loosed, not by the smith but by the Lord! Oh feet blessedly bound, which are guided to paradise in the way of salvation! Oh feet bound for the present time in the world, that they may be always free with the Lord!

Let cruelty, either ignorant or malignant, hold you here in its bonds and chains as long as it will, from this earth and from these sufferings you shall speedily come to the kingdom of heaven. The body is not cherished in the mines with couch and cushions, but it is cherished with the refreshment and solace of Christ. . . . Your limbs unbathed, are foul and disfigured with filth and dirt; but within [internally] they are spiritually cleansed, although without [externally] the flesh is defiled. There the bread is scarce; but man liveth not by bread alone, but by the word of God. Shivering, you want clothing; but he who puts on Christ is both abundantly clothed and adorned. . . . This temporal and brief suffering, how shall it be exchanged for the reward of a bright and eternal honor, when, according to the word of the blessed apostle, "the Lord shall change the body of our humiliation, that it may be fashioned like to the body of His brightness!"

What now must be . . . the loftiness of your mind, what exultation in feeling, what triumph in your breast, that every one of you stands near to the promised reward of God, . . . that you know that Christ is present with you, rejoicing in the endurance of His servants. . . . And now because your word is more effectual in prayers, . . . seek more eagerly. . . that from this darkness and these snares of the world God would set us free with you, sound and glorious; that we . . . may rejoice together in the heavenly kingdom. I bid you, most blessed and most beloved brethren, ever farewell in the Lord, and always and everywhere remember me.[4]

5

The Wonder of Christ

ORIGEN (c. 185–254)

Many times Christians have described devotion to God in terms of a warm heart and an empty head. Since intellectual pursuits lead only to hell, they say, the safe course demands that we shun all scholarship in the interest of devotion to Christ and personal salvation.

However, Christian history offers us a wealth of examples to the contrary. A disciplined mind is neither a sign of God's favor nor a guarantee of his disfavor. Scores of Christian saints have used their minds to express their worship of God. One of these was the third-century genius Origen.

It may seem a bit strange to find Origen in a devotional book. Most people who know him consider him to be an intellectual giant, not a great soul. But his students knew better. And it is this student impact, as well as his long-range influence on Eastern Orthodoxy, that warrants his inclusion here.

Origen refused to accept the common separation of head from heart. He believed that people's thirst for knowledge was traceable to none other than God. When a person sees some admirable work of art, said Origen, he wants to know the rhyme and reason for the creation. The same is true when a person views the works of God. "This desire, this passion, has without doubt been implanted in us by God." This understanding provided the foundation for Origen's enormous intellectual accomplishments.

The shadow of suffering, however, fell across Origen's life and helped to make him a saint as well as a scholar. Shortly after A.D. 200, a persecution against Christians broke out in Alexandria, Egypt, where Origen was raised. His father Leonides, a Christian, was killed in the purge, and the danger of enduring a similar fate drove the city's leading Christian teacher, Clement, from the city. Origen, though only eighteen years of age, stepped into both responsibilities. To support his family he sold his secular books and began his extraordinary career as teacher and scholar.

For the next half century Origen was the most influential figure in the Christian church. He taught in Alexandria; he lectured in Caesarea; he visited Athens. But in any city he was a magnetic teacher, drawing students from hundreds of miles to capture something of his wisdom.

Among these disciples was a young law student from Asia Minor named Gregory. After five years under Origen's instruction, Gregory wrote a book to praise his teacher. Origen, he said, from the first set before the student the goal of genuine philosophy, the attainment of the good life. The good is what man ought to seek; evil is what man ought to flee. The great barrier to godliness, however, is ignorance. We will find no genuine piety toward God in the one who despises the gift of wisdom, but true philosophy always centers on the Word of God, "who attracts all irresistibly to himself by his unutterable beauty."

Origen's own attraction to Jesus Christ is clear in this passage from his major theological work called *On First Principles*.

MAJESTY WITHIN LIMITS

Of all the marvelous and splendid things about the Son of God there is one that utterly transcends the limits of human wonder and is beyond the capacity of our weak mortal intelligence to think of or understand, namely, how this mighty power of the divine majesty, the very Word of the Father, and the very Wisdom of God, in which were created "all things visible and invisible," can be believed to have existed within the compass of that man who appeared in Judaea; yes, and how the wisdom of God can have entered into a woman's womb and been born as a child and uttered noises like those of crying children; and further, how it was that he was troubled, as we are told, in the hour of death, as he himself confesses when he says, "My soul is sorrowful even unto death"; and how at the last he was led to that death which is considered by men to be the most shameful of all,—even though on the third day he rose again.

When, therefore, we see in him some things so human that they appear in no way to differ from the common frailty of mortals, and some things so divine that they are appropriate to nothing else but the . . . nature of deity, the human understanding with its narrow limits is baffled, and struck with amazement at so mighty a wonder knows not which way to turn, what to hold to, or whither to betake itself. If it thinks of God, it sees a man; if it thinks of a man, it beholds one returning from the dead with spoils after vanquishing the kingdom of death.

For this reason we must pursue our contemplation with all fear and reverence, as we seek to prove how the reality of each nature exists in one and the same person, in such a way that nothing unworthy or unfitting may be thought to reside in that divine and ineffable existence, nor on the other hand may the events of his life be supposed to be the illusions caused by deceptive fantasies.

But to utter these things in human ears and to explain them by words far exceeds the powers we possess either in our mortal worth or in mind and speech. I think indeed that it transcends the capacity even of the holy apostles; nay more, perhaps the explanation of this mystery lies beyond the reach of the whole creation of heavenly things.[5]

The Image of God

6

GREGORY OF NYSSA (330–c. 395)

J ames Kidd was a lonely man. He lived on the edge of deprivation. He spent most of his life in a rugged copper mining town in Arizona. But Kidd was troubled by one of the ageless problems facing man. On the second day of 1946 he sat down and wrote out his will. Four years later he disappeared and was never heard from again.

Authorities responsible for the settlement of his will, sixteen years after his disappearance, discovered that he had left almost $200,000 for "research for some scientific proof of a soul of a human body which leaves at death."

How do we know that we are immortal souls? Among the early Christians was a pastor in Asia Minor (today's Turkey) who felt that he had at least a partial answer for people like James Kidd. His name was Gregory of Nyssa. Historians have come to respect him as one of the leading theologians of the early church, because he made an enormous contribution to the orthodox understanding of the holy Trinity. But he was also a trusted spiritual guide.

Gregory was one of the three "Cappadocian Fathers." The other two were his older brother Basil, and Basil's close friend, Gregory of Nazianzus. Temperamentally, Gregory stood in the shadow of his older brother. He sometimes refers to Basil as "the Master." We can understand such a title when we consider the way he followed Basil's lead.

A shy, studious type, Gregory started his public life as a teacher of rhetoric, but when he discovered that Basil was displeased by his entrance into secular life, he repented and entered a monastery founded by Basil. Later, he also accepted somewhat reluctantly, Basil's invitation to become bishop, or pastor, of the church at Nyssa.

The 370s were trouble-filled years in that part of the Roman Empire. When Constantine accepted Christianity as the one true religion, he expected Christians to provide the spiritual and moral cement for the vast empire. But he discovered that they were often divided among themselves over certain essential doctrines.

In Gregory's time no one in the eastern half of the empire could escape the controversy swirling about the question of the Son's relation to the Father.

Gregory opposed the Arians who insisted that the Word, or the Son, was less than fully God. At the Council of Constantinople in 381, called by the emperor to settle the controversy, Gregory not only delivered the inaugural address but also saw his orthodox views triumph.

During these days of controversy Gregory wrote a number of devotional works. In them he taught that human beings have an inclination toward God. James Kidd's search for proof of the soul is itself a reflection of this propensity. And this propensity is what Gregory means by "the image of God." It is marred and defaced, but it is nevertheless there in every person, reflecting the goodness or virtue of God. So the spiritual life, for Gregory, is a perpetual ascent toward the goodness of God.

Gregory's writings often reflect his allegorical use of Scripture and his mystical tone. In this excerpt from his sermons on the Beatitudes he explains what he means by restoring the image of God.

UNDER A VICIOUS COATING

In our human existence physical health is a good thing; and indeed it is a blessing not only to know the reasons for good health but actually to enjoy it. Now suppose a man should speak the praises of good health and then proceed to take food that was unwholesome and contained unhealthy juices. What good would his praise of health be, when he himself was afflicted with disease?

Analogously, then, . . . the Lord does not say that it is blessed to know something about God, but rather to possess God in oneself: Blessed are the clean of heart, for they shall see God (Matthew 5:8). By this I do not think He means that the man who purifies the eye of the soul will enjoy immediate vision of God; rather, I think this marvelous saying teaches us the same lesson that the Word expressed more clearly to others when He said: The kingdom of God is within you (Luke 17:21). And this teaches us that the man who purifies his heart of every creature and every passionate impulse will see the image of the divine nature in his own beauty. So, too, in this short sentence the Word, I think, is giving us the following advice: All you mortals who have within yourselves a desire to behold the supreme Good, when you are told that the majesty of God is exalted above the heavens, that the divine glory is inexpressible, its beauty indescribable, its nature inaccessible, do not despair at never being able to behold what you desire. For you have within your grasp the degree of the knowledge of God which you can attain. For, when God made you, He at once endowed your nature with this perfection: upon the structure of your nature He imprinted an imitation of the perfections of His own nature, just as one would impress upon wax the outline of an emblem. But the wickedness that has been poured all over this divine engraving has made your perfection useless and hidden it with a vicious coating. You must then wash away, by a life of virtue, the dirt that has come to cling to your heart like plaster, and then your divine beauty will once again shine forth.

The same thing is wont to happen with iron. Though it might once have been black, as soon as it has been cleaned of rust with a whetstone it begins to shine and glisten and give off rays in the sun. . . .

It is just like men who look at the sun in a mirror. Even though they do not look up directly at the heavens, they do see the sun in the mirror's reflection just as much as those who look directly at the sun. So it is, says our Lord, with you. Even though you are not strong enough to see the light itself, yet you will find within yourselves what you are seeking, if you will but return to the grace of that image which was established within you from the beginning. For the Godhead is all purity, freedom from passion, the absence of evil. And if you possess these qualities, God will surely be within you. When your mind is untainted by any evil, free of passion, purified of all stain, then you will be blessed because your eye is clear. Then, because you have been purified, you will perceive things that are invisible to the unpurified. The dark cloud of matter will be removed from the eye of your soul, and then you will see clearly that blessed vision within the pure brilliance of your own heart. And what is this vision? It is purity, holiness, simplicity, and other such brilliant reflections of the nature of God, for it is in these things that God is seen.[6]

7
Love for God

AURELIUS AUGUSTINE (354–430)

Human love is almost always *for* something. "Give me," we say, "and I'll love you," or "Love me and I'll love you." Often parents, who ought to know better, stoop to this level. "Be a good boy and I'll love you," or "Do what I say and I'll love you."

God's love, in stark contrast, is always for nothing. Nothing in any of us can arouse it, and nothing in us can destroy it. His love is for nothing.

No one has probed the depths of our loves quite like Saint Augustine, that early Christian intellectual giant who, in his early life, was an unlikely candidate for sainthood.

Perhaps the most famous quotation from Augustine comes early in his *Confessions:* "You have made us for yourself, and our hearts are restless till they find their rest in you." It is a fit summary of one of the best known devotional works ever written: God's sovereign plan and man's endless frustration apart from the grace of God.

Having lived in turbulent times, Augustine witnessed the stream of refugees into North Africa in A.D. 410 after the barbarian Goths had plundered Rome, the imperial capital. He shared the shock of those who discovered that the eternal city was not eternal after all.

He contended, however, that the greatest human crisis is neither political nor social, it is spiritual. He believed this because he knew something about the wickedness of his own heart and the relentless grace of God.

Augustine grew up in North Africa, not far from Carthage, under the watchful eye of a Christian mother, Monica. During his school years, however, he rejected Christianity in favor of other philosophies. He was especially attracted to Manicheism, a belief that the world was created by an evil power opposed to God. But the driving force in Augustine's life was not truth; it was lust.

In 383, he went to Rome to pursue his career as a teacher of rhetoric and gained an appointment in Milan. There he met Bishop Ambrose, and under his influence the relentless Augustine found his spiritual rest. After Monica died, he returned to North Africa and was soon made bishop of Hippo, a little town on the coast of the Mediterranean, west of Carthage.

For over forty years Augustine studied, preached, debated and wrote. He was probably the most influential Christian leader in his time, certainly the most admired in the Middle Ages. When the Roman Empire began to disintegrate around him, Augustine wrote his monumental interpretation of history, *The City of God.* His smaller *Confessions,* however, found a special place in Christian devotional writings. It created an entirely new kind of literature, the spiritual autobiography. Here is a taste of it: Augustine's reflections on love.

A KIND OF FRAGRANCE

I love you, Lord, not doubtingly, but with absolute certainty. Your Word beat upon my heart until I fell in love with you, and now the universe and everything in it tells me to love you, and tells the same thing to us all, so that we are without excuse.

And what do I love when I love you? Not physical beauty, or the grandeur of our existence in time, or the radiance of light that pleases the eye, or the sweet melody of old familiar songs, or the fragrance of flowers and ointments and spices, or the taste of manna or honey, or the arms we like to use to clasp each other. None of these do I love when I love my God. Yet there is a kind of light, and a kind of melody, and a kind of fragrance, and a kind of food, and a kind of embracing, when I love my God. They are the kind of light and sound and odor and food and love that affect the senses of the inner man. There is another dimension of life in which my soul reflects a light that space itself cannot contain. It hears melodies that never fade with time. It inhales lovely scents that are not blown away by the wind. It eats without diminishing or consuming the supply. It never gets separated from the embrace of God and never gets tired of it. That is what I love when I love my God.

And what is my God? I asked the earth and it replied, "I am not he"; and everything in it said the same thing. I asked the sea . . . I asked the heavens, the sun, the moon and stars. They said to me, "Neither are we the God you seek." I said to all the sensory objects that cluster around my body and cause it to react, "You speak of God and say you are not he. Then tell me something about him." And they all cried out with a loud voice, "He made us!" I questioned them by fixing my attention on them, and their beauty was their answer.

Then I turned to myself and said, "Who are you?" And I replied, "A man." But in me are present both body and soul, one exterior, the other interior. Which should I impress to help me find my God? With my physical apparatus I had already searched for him from earth to sky, as far as the eye could see. But the interior equipment is better. The messengers of my body delivered to it the answer of heaven and earth and everything in them when they told me,

"We are not God," and "He made us." The inner man knows these things by means of the ministering of the outer man. The inner "I" knows them; I, the soul, know them through the senses of the body. So I ask the whole frame of the universe about God and it answered back, "I am not he, but he made me."

The truth is, there is one mediator whom you in your hidden mercy have revealed to the meek and lowly, and have sent as an example of humility to be followed. That is the mediator between God and man, the Man Christ Jesus, who has appeared between mortal sinners and the immortal Just One. As men are, he was mortal; as God is, he was just. And because righteousness issues in life and peace, he, through his righteousness with God, nullified the death of justified sinners by sharing their lot with them. . . .

How much you loved us, Good Father, who spared not your own Son but gave him up for us sinners! How much you loved us, since it was on our behalf that he, who thought it no robbery to be equal with you, submitted himself to the death of the cross. He alone was free among the dead because he was free to lay down his life to take it again. For us he was both victor and victim, or should I say, victor because victim. . . . By being born your Son, and then becoming a slave to serve us, he made us to become your sons. So I have good reason for my strong hope in him who sits at your right hand and makes intercession for us. If I didn't have that hope I would be desperate. But I believe that in him you heal all my weaknesses, and they are many and great . . . but your medicine is even greater. It would be easy to think that your Word is too remote for any communication with man. It would be easy to despair, had not the Word become flesh to dwell in our midst.[7]

Part 2

Saints in the Middle Ages

O ne night, early in the fourth century, Anthony, the most revered of early monks, was standing in the desert engaged in earnest prayer. Satan seized the opportunity to rally the wild beasts of the area to send them against Anthony. As they surrounded him, ready to pounce, he looked at them boldly and said, "If you have received power over me from the Lord, then don't delay. I am ready for you. But if you come at the command of Satan, go back to where you come from, for I am a servant of Jesus the Conqueror."

The story came from Athanasius, Bishop of Alexandria, who wrote the popular *Life of Anthony,* but the vision of spiritual power could have come from a thousand of these heroes of the desert. All the essential elements of Christian devotion in the Middle Ages are here: a vivid sense of supernatural reality, the sharp contrast between good and evil, and the courageous soul defying evil and choosing good.

In our world of "sex, power and money," we probably feel a long way from monastic cells, hours of silence, and encounters with the Devil. But are we? In our times the literature of the death camps and the Gulag has a certain similarity to the stories of the early monks. Today's struggle with the demonic is just as fierce and just as real as Saint Anthony's with the Tempter. Which of us lives without temptation, spiritual dryness, and fears of death? Struggles of the soul are much the same in every age.

Perhaps, then, there is a lesson or two for us in the regimen of these spiritual athletes of the Middle Ages. To learn from these ascetics, however, we need some explanations. Why did monks and nuns—or as they are often called "the religious"—arise? The answer lies in the broader history of the church.

THE TIMES

When the Roman Emperor Constantine converted to Christianity early in the fourth century and began to use the church as the social cement of the empire, many Christians were troubled by the church's deepening involvement in worldly wealth and power. Some of these restless souls were driven into the wilderness in search of their personal salvation. That was the beginning for "monks."

These drop-outs from acceptable society appeared first in the deserts of Egypt. Late in the third century, they began settling in isolated caves determined to deny themselves and to battle the Devil in the wilderness, just as Christ had done in Judea. They decided that it was impossible to glorify God surrounded by the temptations and diversions of the city. Alone in the desert, they took up their crosses to follow Christ.

After an initial period marked by extreme austerity, monasticism was tamed and organized. Pachomius, a former soldier, saw the dangers of every hermit doing what was right in his own eyes. He knew that a Christian cannot follow Christ alone but needs to love and submit to others in some kind of community. So he created the first Christian monastery. While allowing plenty of time for private meditation and prayer, he established a regulated common life, in which the monks ate, labored, and worshiped together.

From these beginnings in Egypt, ascetic movements spread to Syria, Asia Minor, and eventually throughout Europe and the world. The most significant of these in Europe was the order called Benedictines after the founder of the movement, Benedict of Nursia (480–547). But reform followed reform: Cluniacs, Cistercians, Franciscans, Dominicans, and Carmelites.

At first, officials in the churches considered the monks extremists, but later their popularity prevailed and they were integrated into the ongoing life of the churches. Their world-denying lifestyle, however, was a silent rebuke for priests and people who remained active in the world. As a consequence, church leaders searched for some presentation of the Christian life that allowed for world-denying monasticism alongside world-affirming churches. They settled for two distinctive ways of living the Christian life.

For most Christians there was a "lower" form of living, suited for the ordinary conditions of human nature. It allowed for Christian marriage, the care of children, and financial support through business and trade but called for all these responsibilities to be conducted in the fear of God. To assist these ordinary Christians in their walk with God, the church provided its worship, prayers, instruction, and sacraments.

For a select few believers there was a second form of living raised above the ordinary conditions of human nature. This way rejected wedlock, personal possessions, and common means of making a living in favor of a separated life devoted to the worship and service of God. This was the way of "the religious," the monks and nuns.

Both lifestyles were nourished by the Roman Catholic understanding of salvation. Christians in almost every age have held that man is a sinner in need of special grace from God; that Jesus Christ by his sacrifice on the cross has secured the reconciliation of man and God; and that all who receive the benefits of Christ's work are acquitted in God's sight. This much is commonly accepted teaching.

But how does God apply the benefits of Christ's work? The Church of

Rome in the Middle Ages insisted that God instituted special ceremonies and special men to apply the benefits of Christ's work. Faith alone in Christ is not enough. Christians need the constant infusion of "cooperating grace" to stimulate Christian virtues in the soul and thus produce those good works that please God.

Thus, in Roman Catholicism saving grace comes to people primarily through the channel of divinely appointed sacraments committed to the keeping of divinely appointed priests within the visible, organized Church of Rome led by the pope. This is the view of salvation that came to dominate the Middle Ages because it was the view of the Church of Rome that shaped events during that time. Let me explain.

Early in the fifth century, a cloud of dust arose on the southern Russian plains. People in the villages peered anxiously toward the east. Was it the wind? No. It was, as they feared, the pounding hooves of horses, driven by yellow, hairless men armed with bows and arrows. The Huns were coming!

Carnage and slaughter soon followed. And then just as quickly as they had come, they were gone, off to other villages to the west. Once, the Huns had been the curse of China, but when they were driven out, they became the scourge of Europe.

Other tribes on the borders of the Roman Empire—the Germans—were driven across the Danube River, and the disintegration of the Empire in the West began. In 410 Rome itself, the Eternal City, hub of the known world, fell into the hands of these uncivilized people. By mid-century Rome was plundered a second time, and in 476 the last Roman emperor in the West surrendered civil authority to a barbarian chief. The fall of the Roman Empire!

What we now call Europe, a loosely allied family of nations, arose like a phoenix from the blazing ruins of this devastated empire in the West. And more than any other force, it was Christianity that brought life and order out of the chaos.

In the next three centuries the church in the West enlisted dedicated monks to serve as a spiritual militia for winning the barbarians to the Christian faith. It looked to the Bishop of Rome, the most influential surviving heir of the Roman tradition, to provide some stable structure for a new way of life. And it turned to the ideals of Christian theology to maintain a framework of spiritual meaning.

Today we think of the Christian faith as deeply personal, something akin to our checkbook or toothbrush. In the Middle Ages, however, Christians thought and lived differently. They came to believe that Christianity was the only true religion and should be the foundation of all public life. It should inspire expressions of art, justify going to war, provide a philosophy of education, and determine policies of the state. The Middle Ages gave us not simply a faith but a unique culture more overtly Christian than any other known to man. And at the center of it was the Church of Rome.

Though never free from its own struggle with the temptations of wealth and power, monasticism served as a warning to a Church in constant danger of deadly compromise with the world. It knew, in a way the official Church did not know, that with God it is "not by might, nor by power, but by my Spirit, says the Lord Almighty."

The monastic alternative to worldly success was spiritual fulfillment. Over the years aspiring monks developed the idea of the soul's progression toward personal holiness. In most monastic disciplines, the soul rises to communion with God by passing through three stages: First, it gains freedom from sin by penance and self-denial; then, it forms basic spiritual virtues by prayer and the imitation of Christ; and finally, it advances in the love of God until it reaches habitual union with the High and Holy One.

We might think of saints in the monastic tradition as spiritual athletes. They give themselves to a rigorous training program, thereby foregoing many of life's pleasures, because they know that their future spiritual victories will make any personal sacrifice seem as nothing.

Monasticism, however, contained a fatal flaw. It ran counter to the Christian doctrine of creation. It said that man's basic problem is his flesh and that marriage is evil and to be avoided at all costs.

The Bible, however, says that when God looked at creation he saw that it was good. God himself made woman for man and man for woman. Man's basic problem, then, is not the body per se, but his alienated affections. He loves himself, his opinions and his pleasures, more than he loves God. This self-love is, in fact, so deeply rooted in the human heart that only God himself can pluck it out and replace it with love for God.

In the five chapters that follow, we can discover a few of the ways that saints in the monastic movement trained their souls in godliness and expressed their devotion to God.

Training in Godliness

BENEDICT OF NURSIA (480–547)

Here is a verse from one of Isaac Watt's well-known hymns.

> See how we grovel here below
> Fond of these earthly toys.
> Our souls, how heavily they go,
> To reach eternal joys.

Few Christians would deny the soul's need for change if it is ever to "reach eternal joys." Some say it can happen in a moment of time through the compulsive power of a new affection. Others say it can only happen over a lifetime of rigorous training.

For well over a thousand years, the monastic movement argued for training in godliness. The great mentors for the spiritual life, Basil, John Cassian, Bernard of Clairvaux, Francis of Assisi, and others wrote their "rules," their manuals of discipline, for achieving true spirituality. All of them believed that salvation, like education, came through training, through the restraint of evil, and through the nurture of righteousness. None of these monastic fathers, however, read human nature any more accurately or designed his spiritual lessons any more effectively than Benedict of Nursia, tutor of the Benedictines.

Nursia, Benedict's hometown, was about eighty-five miles northeast of Rome, close enough to share the fortunes and the influence of the once proud capital. In Benedict's day this meant the ravages of the barbarian invasions and the longing for ordered life under the rule of law.

Benedict interrupted his education in Rome to pursue an ascetic life in a lonely cave south of the city. He spent three years in the study of Scripture and in severe self-denial until the monks of a neighboring monastery chose him for their abbot or spiritual leader. Benedict's strict discipline, however, proved too irksome, and the monks tried to poison him. Even a return to solitude proved impossible for him in that region.

Benedict got a second chance on the rugged heights of Monte Cassino, eighty-five miles southeast of Rome. In 529, he laid the foundations there for what became the most famous monastery in Europe, the motherhouse of the Benedictine order. He wrote his famous *Rule* (or manual) for his monastery on Monte Cassino, that became the charter for an entire movement.

In the introduction to the *Rule*, Benedict underscores the typical monastic conviction that salvation, like knowledge, comes only as the fruit of disciplined training in godliness, especially in the virtues of poverty, chastity, and obedience.

A SCHOOL FOR BEGINNERS

Son, listen to the precepts of your master; take them to your heart willingly. If you follow the advice of a tender father and travel the hard road of obedience, you will return to God, from whom by disobedience you have gone astray.

I address my discourse to all of you who will renounce your own will, enter the lists under the banner of obedience, and fight under the lead of your lawful sovereign, Christ the Lord.

First, I advise that you should implore the help of God to accomplish every good work you undertake; that he, who has now vouchsafed to rank us in the number of his children, may be no more grieved at our doing amiss. For we ought always to use his grace so faithfully in his service, as to give him no occasion to disinherit his children like an angry parent, or to punish for eternity his servants, like a master incensed at their crimes—servants who have refused to follow him in the way to glory. . . .

Let us then gird up our loins; let us walk by faith and try to serve him with good works; and thereby let us advance in his ways with the Gospel as our guide, that we may deserve to behold him who has called us to his kingdom. If we want to fix our dwelling there, we cannot arrive thereto without running in the ways of virtue. But let us enquire of the Lord with the prophet: "Lord who shall dwell in thy tabernacle, or who shall rest upon thy holy hill?" Brethren, let us hear the Lord's answer to the question, an answer which shows the way to the heavenly tabernacle: "He that walketh without blame and does right; he that speaketh truth in his heart; he that hath kept his tongue from guile, hath done no evil to his neighbor, and hath not believed slander of his neighbor."

When we enquired of the Lord about the person who should dwell in his tabernacle, we were informed what conditions were necessary for it; and it is now ours to perform those conditions. Therefore our hearts and bodies are to be prepared to fight under his command; and we must beseech God to supply with his grace what it is impossible for nature to effect alone. Moreover, if we desire to avoid the pains of hell, and to compass eternal life, we must, while we have time in the body and ability to use the opportunity of a religious life, make haste and practice now the virtues which will serve us for all eternity.

To conclude: I am to erect a school for beginners in the service of the Lord: which I hope to establish on laws not too difficult or grievous. But if, for reasonable cause, for the retrenchment of vice or preservation of charity, I require some things which may seem too austere, you are not thereupon to be frightened from the ways of salvation. Those ways are always strait and narrow at the beginning. But as we advance in the practices of religion and in the faith, the heart insensibly opens and enlarges through the wonderful sweetness of his love, and we run in a way of God's commandments. If then we keep close to our school and the doctrine we learn in it, and persevere in the monastery till death, we shall here share by patience in the passion of Christ and hereafter deserve to be united with him in his kingdom. Amen.[8]

Seeing God

BERNARD OF CLAIRVAUX (1090–1153)

A few years ago friends of ours who had grown up in the Amana community of eastern Iowa gave us a tour of the seven colonies. In South Amana we came upon a well-kept old house, lined on the south side by pink petunias and red begonias. At the west end of the flowerbed was a tiny sign and a bit of verse. It read:

The kiss of the sun for pardon,
The song of the bird for mirth,
One is nearer to God's heart in the garden
Than any place else on earth.

Saints tell us that they have often talked with God in their gardens. "Talking" with God and "seeing" God are ways Christians describe their communion with God. Seeing God is the way believers describe heaven and the life to come. The idea comes from the Bible itself. In the Book of Revelation we read: "The throne of God and of the Lamb will be in the city, and his servants will serve him. They will see his face, . . ." (Revelation 22:3–4).

But what can seeing God possibly mean? In one of his best-known works, a series of sermons *On the Song of Solomon,* Bernard of Clairvaux tells us what he believes "seeing God" means.

In the late Middle Ages, few would question Bernard's knowledge of such things. He was one of the most admired men of the period. In Dante's *Divine Comedy,* for example, we find Bernard not only in Paradise, but in the very presence of God!

Bernard grew up near Dijon, France, under the proud glances of a knightly father and a devout mother. At twenty-two years of age along with thirty companions, he entered the Cistercian monastery at Citeaux. Three years later his superiors asked him to establish a new community at Clairvaux. Bernard's reputation soon made Clairvaux the principal center of the whole movement. He was personally responsible for establishing sixty-five new monastic houses!

Bernard, however, was more than a dedicated monk. He was both a contemplative mystic and a social activist. He opposed Peter Abelard's liberal ideas; he healed a papal schism in 1130; and he was charged with preaching the Second Crusade. He was easily the most powerful figure of the twelfth century.

To this day many Christians find several of Bernard's hymns, including "Jesus, the Very Thought of Thee," appropriate expressions of their own aspirations. One of these hymns is especially fitting as an introduction to Bernard's thoughts about seeing God.

Jesus, Thou joy of loving hearts,
Thou Fount of life, Thou light of men,
From the best bliss that earth imparts
We turn unfilled to Thee again.

We taste Thee, O Thou living bread,
And long to feast upon Thee still;
We drink of Thee, Thou Fountainhead,
And thirst, our souls from Thee to fill.

O Jesus, ever with us stay;
Make all our moments calm and bright;
Chase the dark night of sin away;
Shed o'er the world Thy holy light.

This is the way Bernard explains what it means to "see" God.

AFFLICTED WITH LONGINGS

The Word, who is the Bridegroom, frequently appears to zealous souls under more than one form. Why is this? I think doubtless it is because we are not able to see Him as He really is (1 John 3:2). Only in heaven is the form of Him abiding, because the form in which we shall know Him will then also be permanent. . . .

Those who would behold God neither desire, nor are capable of beholding anything more desired than Him. When, then, can the eagerness of their gaze be satiated, the sweetness in which they delight be withdrawn, or the truth be exhausted? In a word, when can eternity come to an end?

Such a beatific vision is not for the present life, but is reserved for the final state of existence. It is reserved for those, at least, who are able to say: "We know that when He shall appear we shall be like Him, for we shall see Him as He is" (1 John 3:2). Even in the present life He appears to whom He wills, but in the manner as He wills, not as He is. There is no man, however wise or holy, there is no prophet who is or ever was able to see Him in this mortal body as He is. Yet those who shall be found worthy shall do so when their bodies shall be immortal.

Therefore He is indeed seen, but in a manner that seems good unto Him and not as He is. For though you have seen that great luminary, that is the sun which you behold every day, you have never seen it as it really is, but only as it lights up other things. . . .

In the present sphere of existence you discern something of Him by the great variety of created forms of life. They are like the rays of the Sun of the Divine Being, showing indeed that He exists, from whom they derive their existence. This fact of His existence should lead you forward to seek further after Him. . . .

Again the patriarchs saw God manifested in another form. For He granted to them frequent and familiar communion with His presence, even though He was not actually visible to them as He really is, but only as He designed to appear to them. . . .

But there is still another manner in which God was seen. It differed from the others in that it was inward. It was the way in which God deigned of His own accord to make Himself known to a soul that sought longingly for Him . . . After a soul has been thus pressed by such frequent aspirations after God, or rather by such continual prayer, and afflicted with those longings, it sometimes happens that God has pity on the soul and makes Himself manifest. I think this was the experience of the prophet Jeremiah when he said: "The Lord is good to them that wait upon the Lord, to the soul that seeks after Him" (Lamentations 3:25). . . .

But be very careful not to allow yourself to think that vision of God will be induced by any imaginary, bodily experience, as the Word and the soul of the believer are so united. I say this, because the apostle reminds us that "He who is joined to the Lord is one spirit" (1 Corinthians 6:17). That union is made in spirit because God is Spirit, and He is moved with love for the beauty of the soul that He sees walking in the Spirit, and he does not desire to live carnally. . . . To such he comes, not with a sound in the ears, but as penetrating the heart. He comes not full of words, but full of power. He comes to the affections as sweetness itself, ineffably so. The features of His countenance are not formed and definable, yet they exercise formative powers. They do not strike upon the vision of the retina, but they rejoice the heart.[9]

10
Perfect Joy

FRANCIS OF ASSISI (1181–1226)

If a picture is worth a thousand words, what shall we say of a life? Isn't example the best teacher? When we consider the turning points in our lives, most of us look back to some person who showed us how to live. In Christian history, a select few spiritual guides have seized this truth and made their lives their message. The supreme instance of this conviction, that living counts for so much more than teaching, is Francis of Assisi.

Giovanni Francesco Bernardone, known to us as Francis of Assisi, grew up in a twelfth-century, wealthy Italian home as a popular but self-indulgent child. His father had dreams that his son would some day succeed him in the management of his clothing business. Dreams, however, turned to nightmares of disappointment when Francis renounced his riches and followed a persistent call to preach the virtues of poverty.

Francis left his family but gained a following. His winsome preaching to the poor proved magnetic. His companions came to be called the Friars Minor, monks who supported their preaching ministry by begging, because they were convinced that is the way that Jesus and his apostles lived. We call the movement the "Franciscans."

Francis left us practically nothing from his pen. He knew the sins of authors. His message was in his joyous life of humility and poverty. He served the poor, kissed the leper, talked to the animals, and sang the praises of the wind and sun.

Almost as soon as Francis submitted to "Sister Death," however, his followers began publishing supposed incidents from his life. These biographical snapshots—called "Little Flowers" or *Fioretti,* meaning "anthology" in the medieval Italian—are a blend of legend and fact. Most historians consider them elaborate embellishments of an authentic tradition within the early Franciscans. What we should look for in reading them is not history but the ideal virtues of the early Franciscan movement: humility, simplicity, poverty, and prayer.

Here is one of the "Little Flowers," an example of hundreds of others.

GLORY IN CONTEMPT

One day in the winter, as St. Francis was coming to St. Mary of the Angels from Perugia with Brother Leo, who was walking a bit ahead of him, and he said: "Brother Leo, even if the Friars Minor in every country should give a great example of holiness and integrity and good edification, nevertheless write down and note carefully that perfect joy in not in that."

And going on a bit, St. Francis cried out again in a strong voice: "Brother Leo, if a Friar Minor knew all languages and all sciences and Scripture, if he also knew how to prophesy and to reveal not only the future but also the secrets of the consciences and minds of others, write down and note carefully that perfect joy is not in that."

Now when he had been talking this way for a distance of two miles, Brother Leo in great amazement asked him: "Father, I beg you in God's name to tell where perfect joy is."

And St. Francis replied: "When we come to St. Mary of the Angels, soaked by the rain and frozen by the cold, all soiled with mud and suffering from hunger, and we ring at the gate of the Place and the brother porter comes and says angrily: 'Who are you?' And we say: 'We are two of your brothers.' And he contradicts us saying: 'You are not telling the truth. Rather, you are two rascals who go around deceiving people and stealing what they give to the poor. Go away! And he does not open the door for us, but makes us stand outside in the snow and rain, cold and hungry, until night falls—then if we endure all those insults and cruel rebuffs patiently, without being troubled and without complaining, and if we reflect humbly and charitably that that porter really knows us and God makes him speak against us, oh, Brother Leo, write that perfect joy is there! . . .

"And if later, suffering intensely from hunger and the painful cold, with night falling, we still knock and call, and crying loudly beg them to open for us and let us come in for the love of God, and he grows still more angry and says: 'Those fellows are bold and shameless ruffians. I'll give them what they deserve!' And he comes out with a knotty club, and grasping us by the cowl throws us to the ground, rolling us in the mud and snow, and beats us with that club so much that he covers our bodies with wounds—if we endure all those evils and insults and blows with joy and patience, reflecting that we must accept and bear the sufferings of the Blessed Christ patiently for love of Him, oh, Brother Leo, write: that is perfect joy!

"And now hear the conclusion, Brother Leo. Above all the graces and the gifts of the Holy Spirit which Christ grants to His friends is that of conquering oneself and willingly enduring sufferings, insults, humiliations, and hardships for the love of Christ. For we cannot glory in all those other marvelous gifts of

God, as they are not ours but God's, as the Apostle says: 'What have you that you have not received?' "

But we can glory in the cross of tribulations and afflictions, because that is ours, and so the Apostle says: "I will not glory save in the Cross of our Lord Jesus Christ!"[10]

Page 58

11

Taking Faith Seriously

GERMAN THEOLOGY (late fourteenth century)

Over the years, Christianity has probably suffered more from half-hearted followers than from hard-headed scoffers. Complacent Christianity is simply a contradiction. And yet most of us have seen more than our share of it, not only in others, but in our own lives.

The problem is as old as the church itself. In one of the letters to the seven churches of Asia, the letter to the Laodiceans, the Lord says, " 'I know your deeds, that you are neither cold nor hot. I wish you were either one or the other! So, because you are lukewarm—neither hot nor cold—I am about to spit you out of my mouth' " (Revelation 3:15–16).

What does it mean to take the Christian faith with utmost seriousness? An anonymous work from the late fourteenth century attempted to answer that question.

Theologia Germanica, or as it is in English *German Theology,* was a favorite of Martin Luther because it confirmed his own evangelical experience of the grace of God. He demonstrated his appreciation for the little book by publishing a short version of it in 1516 and the entire book in 1518. But Luther is far from alone in his admiration.

The book expresses the ideals of a movement. Out of the turmoil of the late Middle Ages came several revivals for the spiritual life. One of these in the fourteenth century was a monastic awakening called "The Friends of God." The Friends rejected religion based on fear of punishment or promises of rewards, in favor of faith based on a personal experience of God's presence.

Perhaps the medieval mystic Meister Eckhart and certainly the Dominican priest John Tauler were among the Friends of God. Both of them emphasized in their sermons the importance of a personal life of prayer and faith, but *German Theology* is probably the best antidote to "complacent Christianity" the Friends of God have left us.

TWO TRUSTWORTHY PATHS

Christ's soul had to visit hell before it came to heaven. This is also the path for man's soul. . . .

When a person comes to know and see himself, he discovers that he is wicked and unworthy of the goodness and comfort that he has received from God and from fellow beings. He then feels that he is damned and lost and unworthy even of that. Yes, he thinks that he is unworthy of the sufferings that he may undergo in his earthly life. He thinks that it is mete and right that all creatures should turn against him and cause him suffering and agony and that he is unworthy of this, too.

He also deems it right that he should be eternally damned and be a footstool for all the devils in hell and, again, that he is unworthy even of that.

He cannot or does not want to ask for comfort or deliverance from either God or man. Rather, he wants to remain uncomforted and unsaved, and he does not regret his damnation and his sufferings since he judges them mete and just and not contrary to God but in accordance with the will of God. In his view this is right; he is resigned to it.

Only his guilt and wickedness make for grief in his heart. For his guilt and his wickedness are not right, they are contrary to God. Hence this gives him pain and troubles his spirit.

It is this that we call true contrition over sin. . . .

Now God does not leave man in this hell. No, He takes him to Himself and the result is that man does not ask for anything but the eternal Good alone and knows that the eternal Good is exceedingly precious. Yes, it becomes his ecstasy, his peace, his joy, his rest, his fullness.

And when man asks for and demands nought but the eternal Good, and nothing for himself, then he comes into the possession of the eternal Good and knows peace, joy, ecstasy, delight, and such. Thus man is in the kingdom of heaven.

This experience of hell and heaven is like two trustworthy paths for man in his earthly life, and happy is the person who travels on them properly and well.

For finally hell departs but the kingdom of heaven will remain.

It is important to note again that when a person is in this hell, nothing can comfort him and he cannot believe that he will ever be delivered and comforted.

But when he is in heaven nothing can trouble or overwhelm him. He cannot understand how anything could trouble or discomfort him. . . .

When a person is in one of these two conditions he is on the right road. He can be as safe in hell as in heaven. As long as man is on earth, in a temporal state, he might pass frequently from one to the other, indeed perhaps even during a single day or a single night—and without his own doing.

But when man is in neither of these conditions, he clings too closely to created beings and wavers hither and thither and knows not what he is doing. He should therefore never forget the two roads in his heart.[11]

12

The Vanity of the World

THOMAS A KEMPIS (c. 1380–1471)

Karl Heim, the Lutheran theologian, said in one of his books, "What Jesus wants is not admirers, but disciples." It was a helpful distinction. We have today, as in every day, a host of admirers of Jesus. But disciples, those who conform their lives to his, are harder to find.

How does a true disciple live? One book from the close of the fourteenth century dared to answer that question. Its title is almost shocking—*The Imitation of Christ*. In spite of its apparent presumption, however, *The Imitation* is probably the favorite devotional guide, apart from the Bible, among Christians of all nationalities, creeds, and times.

Who actually wrote this popular little volume is debated. We know that it came from a movement for spiritual renewal called the Brethren of the Common Life. These devout laymen in Holland were apparently stimulated in their Christian faith by the preaching of Gerard Groote. They banded together to encourage one another in personal obedience to Christ and in the education of young people.

Some of the Brethren remained laymen well into the fifteenth century, but some of them also formed religious, or monastic type, houses. In one of these, Mt. St. Agnes near Swolle, Thomas à Kempis was a copyist and a spiritual advisor.

As a product of the Brethren school at Deventer, Thomas was well trained in the ideals of the movement. After ordination to the priesthood in 1413, he assumed more leadership in Mt. St. Agnes, where his brother had been. Thomas gave himself to the ministry of spiritual guidance and to his work as a copyist. For over five centuries, however, Christians have linked his name with *The Imitation*. It seems clear that he did edit and publish the work, but some scholars contend that Gerard Groote, before his death in 1374, actually wrote the little book.

Thankfully, readers of *The Imitation* today, like those in earlier generations, can profit from the content of the book without a resolution of the debate over authorship. The best advice seems to be the psalmist's: "Oh, taste and see . . . "

ROOTING OUT THE VICES

"He that followeth Me, walketh not in darkness," saith the Lord. These are the words of Christ, by which we are taught to imitate His life and manners, if we would be truly enlightened, and be delivered from all blindness of heart. Let therefore our chief endeavor be to meditate upon the life of Jesus Christ. . . .

If thou knewest the whole Bible by heart, and the sayings of the philosophers, what would it profit thee without the love of God and without grace. Vanity of vanities, all is vanity, except to love God, and Him only to serve. . . .

All men naturally desire knowledge; but what availeth knowledge without the fear of God? . . . O, if men bestowed as much labor in the rooting out of vices, and the planting of virtues, as they do in the moving of questions, neither would so many evils be done, nor so great scandal be given in the world. Truly, at the day of judgment we shall not be examined as to what we have read, but as to what we have done; not as to how well we have spoken, but as to how religiously we have lived.

Tell me, where are all those Doctors and Masters, with whom thou wast well acquainted, whilst they lived and flourished in learning? Others occupy their places and perhaps do scarce ever think of those who went before them. In their lifetime they seemed something, but now they are not spoken of. O, how quickly doth the glory of the world pass away! Would that their life had been answerable to their learning! Then had their study and reading been to good purpose.

How many perish by reason of vain learning of this world, who take little care of the serving of God. And because they rather choose to be great than humble, therefore they become vain in their imaginations.

He is truly great who hath great love. He is truly great that is little in himself, and that maketh no account of any height of honor. He is truly wise, that accounteth all earthly things as dung, that he may win Christ. And he is truly learned, that doeth the will of God, and forsaketh his own will. . . .

The glory of a good man is the testimony of a good conscience. . . . Thou art not the more holy for being praised; nor the more worthless for being dispraised. What thou art, that thou art; neither by words canst thou be made greater than what thou art in the sight of God. If thou consider what thou art in thyself, thou wilt not care what men say of thee. Man looketh on the countenance, but God on the heart. . . .

He that seeketh no testimony on his behalf from without, doth show that he hath wholly committed himself unto God. . . .

When thou hast Christ, thou art rich, and hast enough. He will be thy faithful and provident helper in all things, so that thou shalt not need to trust in men. For men soon change, and quickly fail; but Christ remaineth forever, and standeth by us firmly unto the end. . . .

If thou hadst but once perfectly entered into the secrets of the Lord Jesus, and tasted a little of His ardent love; then wouldst thou not regard thine own convenience or inconvenience, but rather wouldst rejoice in reproaches, if they should be cast upon thee; for the love of Jesus maketh a man to despise himself. A lover of Jesus and the truth, and a true inward Christian, and one free from the inordinate affections, can freely turn himself unto God, and lift himself above himself in spirit, and rest in full enjoyment.[12]

Part 3

Saints in the Reformation Era

I n the summer of 1520, a document bearing an impressive seal circulated throughout Germany in search of a remote figure. "Arise, O Lord," the document began, "and judge Thy cause. A wild boar has invaded Thy vineyard."

The bull—named after the seal, or *bulla*—from Pope Leo X took three months to reach Martin Luther, the wild boar. Long before it arrived at the University of Wittenberg, where Luther was teaching, he knew its contents. It called on him to repudiate his errors or face the dreadful consequences, excommunication from "the One, Holy, Catholic, and Apostolic Church."

Luther responded to the threat by leading an eager mob of university students in burning copies of the Church Law, books of some medieval theologians, and the papal bull. Those flames are a fit symbol of the defiance of papal authority that soon raged throughout sixteenth-century Europe, and of the new way of describing saints.

THE TIMES

We call this revolt "The Protestant Reformation." It began as a movement determined to reform the Catholic Church and in the end it changed the face of Christianity. In the sixteenth century, the movement took four major expressions: Lutheranism in northern Germany and Scandinavia; Anabaptism near Zurich and in the Netherlands; the Reformed churches in Geneva, France, Scotland, Hungary, and the Netherlands; and the Anglican Church in England. By the 1540s, the Roman Catholic Church, led by the Jesuits, had its own "reformation," marked by new expressions of austerity and devotion.

At the heart of all these changes in the churches of western Europe was a transformation in the way Christians pictured and practiced the spiritual life. Catholic authorities and Protestant reformers disagreed sharply over several fundamental questions, but the most basic one was, how can a person find God's forgiveness?

The Roman Catholic Church answered, "For ordinary church members two things are necessary: First, as sinners they must repent and confess their sins to a priest in order to receive God's forgiveness for the eternal punishment that leads to hell. Second, by prayers, fasting, good works, and the sacraments, they must remove the temporal punishment that leads to purgatory. In other words, justification before God comes by a combination of faith and good works.

"For those extraordinary people, however, who find no release, no freedom from their sins, and no fellowship with God, there is another way, a second mile, the path of monastic discipline. By submitting to the yoke of poverty, chastity, and obedience, these troubled souls can find freedom from their sins and love for God."

As we have seen, during the Middle Ages the Roman Catholics came to accept two paths to salvation and peace: One in the world of normal human testing—raising a family, making a living, and participating in human society—the other in the cloister, cut off from the world, enduring the regimen of self-denial, pursuing the cultivation of virtues, and loving God.

The Protestant Reformers answered the question of salvation in a sharply different way. They said, "No! A person is justified in God's sight through faith in the Lord Jesus Christ alone. All human works are worthless for obtaining God's forgiveness. Only the death of Jesus Christ is sufficient to pay the enormous debt man owes to God, but anyone who genuinely trusts in Jesus Christ, however poor and needy, can find God's forgiveness.

"The Christian life is essentially a life of gratitude. Self-denial, service, worship, and all the other marks of the spiritual life grow out of justification by faith alone. Sanctity is the fruit of a life rooted in personal faith in Jesus Christ as Savior and Lord."

If that is so, if no spiritual regimen or good work can contribute in any way to one's relationship with God, if faith in Christ and faith alone is the soul's only need, then why retain the whole elaborate monastic way of life? Protestant Christians found no adequate answer to that question, so they removed all distinctions between the spiritual life pursued in the world and out of the world. They completely abandoned monasticism and "the religious life" in the Catholic sense. Gone were the vows, and rules, and walls. Only one standard for the Christian life remained: the calling of God in marriage and the world. Family life moved to the highest levels of spiritual status, and the righteousness of God was offered to everyone equally, in the home and in the world.

The best place to see this transformation is in Martin Luther's life. Growing up in the traditional Catholic home of a Saxon miner, Luther was troubled by an overwhelming sense of estrangement from God. The sacraments, confession of sin, acts of penance—nothing seemed to bring him peace with God. His problem was not his sinful acts, but his sinful condition. He knew that the Church of Rome required him to love God, but in his heart he found only hatred of God. How can you love the judge who condemns you?

In 1505, while attending law school, Luther was caught in a violent thunderstorm. A bolt of lightning knocked him to the ground. Terrified, he cried out to the first saint who came to mind, the patroness of miners: "St. Anne, save me! And I'll become a monk."

Luther kept that vow and entered the Augustinian monastery at Erfurt, determined to make his peace with God. "I kept the rule so strictly," he recalled years later, "that I may say that if ever a monk got to heaven by sheer monkery, it was I."

He drove himself to self-denying extremes. He fasted for three days; he slept without a blanket in freezing winter. But no amount of penance or good works could erase the conviction that he was a miserable, doomed sinner.

Luther found the forgiveness and love he sought through his study of Scripture. Assigned to teach the Bible at the University of Wittenberg, he came upon the apostle's words in Romans 1:17: "The just shall live by faith"(KJV). When Luther saw that the justice of God is that righteousness of God by which he justifies sinners through sheer mercy, and that a sinner can receive God's forgiveness through faith alone, he felt like he had "gone through open doors into paradise."

A flagrant abuse of church finances propelled the monk into public controversy. In exchange for some meritorious work—frequently a contribution to a worthy cause—the Church of Rome offered sinners exemption from their acts of penance by drawing upon a "treasury of merits" made available to the Church by Christ's sacrifice and the meritorious deeds of the saints. This exemption was called an "indulgence."

In 1517, a Dominican monk named John Tetzel came to Germany offering a papal indulgence in exchange for a contribution to the building fund of St. Peter's basilica in Rome. He promised the donors a chance to free souls in purgatory. "As soon as the coin in the coffer rings," Tetzel chanted, "another soul from purgatory springs."

Such crass commercialism drove Luther to his desk to write his *95 Theses,* a list of propositions for theological debate. These he posted on the door of the Castle Church in Wittenberg. The date was October 31, 1517. Within three months, all of Germany knew about the *Theses.*

No one, declared Luther, can truly repent of sin by simply going to a priest and striking a bargain. Only God can remove the punishment of our guilt. The Pope has no power to help a soul in purgatory. Besides, if the Pope could save souls in purgatory, shouldn't he do it out of sheer Christian love rather than for mere monitary gain? These are the kinds of questions that led to his excommunication, to the bonfire at Wittenberg, and to the spread of the Protestant Reformation. Soon all of Europe was aflame with reform.

The Protestant alternative to the Catholic way left some unanswered questions of its own. Justification through faith in Christ alone was clear enough, but what about sanctification, or personal holiness, through the Spirit? Protestants set the Word of God in place of the Roman Catholic priesthood, sacraments, confessional, and devotions surrounding the Mass. The truth of God revealed in the Bible was not only central to worship, it was also communicated to believers beyond public worship by catechism, Bible study, and private prayer. While working obediently in one's earthly calling, the Protestant was continually aware of God's standards, mercy, and forgiveness.

But just exactly what piety in the world looked like and what practical means were available to achieve that piety were often far from clear. Did Protestants prove more successful than Catholics in producing saints? Any final answer to that question seems unlikely in the near future. Like their Catholic neighbors, Protestants were often caught in the trap of prevailing secular standards with their concentration on man's pleasure rather than on God's glory.

In individual lives, however, we can sense the warmth and the light of a fresh experience of the grace of God. In the selections that follow in Part 3, we find some of the ways the reforming spirit found expression in the various Christian traditions: Lutheran, Anabaptist, Reformed, Catholic, and Anglican.

13

Comfort in Distress

MARTIN LUTHER (1483–1546)

The Christian's life alone with God finds many public and interpersonal expressions—corporate worship, social justice, acts of mercy—but none of them reveal the Christian's spiritual perspective any more clearly than the encouragement and counsel he offers his family and friends. Martin Luther was a master at this.

When most of us hear the name "Martin Luther," we probably think of the burly monk who defied the pope or threw an inkwell at the Devil. Usually we think of the Protestant reformer and Bible translator.

Luther was both, but to those who knew him best he was a pastor, a spiritual counselor and guide. Even the event that marks the birth of the Protestant Reformation—Luther's posting of his *95 Theses*—arose out of his pastoral concern for his people who were securing those papal letters of pardon as guarantees of their salvation.

In the sixteenth century the Church of Rome offered people a confident religion. It believed the Lord Jesus Christ had himself created the priestly institution headed by the pope and that God's saving grace was dispensed, almost automatically, to people through this sacred institution and its seven sacraments.

When Luther discovered by studying the Scriptures that God's forgiveness came through personal faith in the Lord Jesus Christ, he had reason to question confidence in any institution. Tetzel's hawking of "indulgences" struck Luther as blatant "cheap grace." Far from providing an aid to salvation, it was, in fact, a barrier to it.

For the next thirty years, while dodging all papal attacks, Luther was able to make this point and to fashion a reformed church in northern Germany, while he served as a pastor and spiritual counselor. We see this side of the reformer best in his letters.

We offer two of Luther's letters here. The first is to a bereaved father, Thomas Zink, whose son John had come to Wittenberg in 1530 to study, but who suddenly died in March, 1532. The second, written in October, 1534, is to Matthias Weller, an employee of Duke Henry of Saxony and an organist, who seems to have had trouble with depression. In both letters, we see Luther's compassion and his down-to-earth use of Scripture.

COMPASSIONATE COUNSEL

Grace and peace in Christ, our Lord.

My dear friend:

By this time I trust you will have learned that your dear son, John Zink, whom you sent here to study, was overtaken by a grave illness and, although nothing was spared in the way of care, attention, and medicine, the disease got the upper hand and carried him off to heaven, to our Lord Jesus Christ. We were all very fond of the boy, who was especially dear to me because I had him in my home many an evening for singing. He was quiet, well-behaved, and diligent in his studies. Accordingly we are all deeply distressed by his death. If it had been possible, we should have been glad to save and keep him. But God loved him even more and desired to have him.

It is only natural that your son's death and the report of it should distress and grieve you and your dear wife, his parents. I do not blame you for this, for all of us, and I in particular, are stricken with sorrow. Yet I admonish you that you should much rather thank God for giving you such a good, pious son and for deeming you worthy of all the pains and money you have invested in him But let this be your best comfort, as it is ours, that he fell asleep (rather than departed) decently and softly with such a fine testimony of his faith on his lips that we all marveled. There can be as little doubt that he is with God, his true Father, in eternal blessedness, as there can be doubt that the Christian faith is true. Such a beautiful Christian end as his cannot fail to lead heavenward. . . .

Grieve in such a way, therefore, as to console yourselves. For you have lost him, but you have only sent him on ahead of you to be kept in everlasting blessedness. Saint Paul says that we should not mourn over the departed, over those who have fallen asleep, like the heathen.

I shall see to it that Master Veit Dietrich, your son's precentor, writes down for you some of the beautiful words which your son uttered before his death. They will please and comfort you. . . .

Christ, our Lord and Comforter, allow me to commit you to his grace. Amen.

Dr. Martin Luther, written with my own
hand although I too am weak.

Grace and peace in Christ.

Honorable, kind, good Friend:

Your dear brother has informed me that you are deeply distressed and
    afflicted with melancholy. He will undoubtedly tell you what I have said
    to him.

*Dear Matthias, do not dwell on your thoughts, but listen to what other people
have to say to you. For God has commanded men to comfort their brethren,
and it is his will that the afflicted should receive such consolation as God's
very own. Thus our Lord speaks through Saint Paul, "Comfort the fainthearted," and through Isaiah: "Comfort ye, comfort ye my people. Speak ye
comfortably. . . ."*

*Listen, then, to what we are saying to you in God's name: Rejoice in Christ,
who is your gracious Lord and Redeemer. Let him bear your burdens, for he
assuredly cares for you, even if you do not yet have all you would like. He still
lives. Look to him for the best. . . .*

*When you are sad, therefore, and when melancholy threatens to get the upper
hand, say: "Arise! I must play a song unto the Lord on my regal [a portable
organ]. . . , for the Scriptures teach us that it pleases him to hear a joyful song
and the music of the stringed instruments." Then begin striking the keys and
singing in accompaniment, as David and Elisha did, until your sad thoughts
vanish. . . .*

*Therefore, the best thing you can do is to rap the devil on the nose at the very
start. Act like the man who, whenever his wife began to nag and snap at him,
drew out his flute from under his belt and played merrily until she was
exhausted and let him alone. So you too must turn to your regal or gather
some good companions about you and sing with them until you learn how to
defy the devil. . . .*

*And when good people comfort you, my dear Matthias, learn to believe that
God is speaking to you through them. Pay heed to them and have no doubt
that it is most certainly God's word, coming to you according to God's
command through men, that comforts you.*

*May the same Lord who told me these things, and whom I obey, communicate
all these things to you in your heart and enable you to believe them. Amen.*

Martin Luther, Doctor

Wednesday after Saint Francis, 1534.[13]

14

To Die is Gain

MARTYRDOM OF MICHAEL SATTLER (c. 1490–1527)

The only gift some Christians have to offer to God is their suffering. This is true of some individuals in our own time. They can not recall a single day without pain. It has also been true of certain Christian groups in the past. We think immediately of the Black church in American slavery, the so-called "invisible institution" with its melancholy spirituals and gospel songs. "Nobody knows the trouble I see. Nobody knows, but Jesus."

The "invisible institution" of the Protestant Reformation was Anabaptism. Like the Black church in slavery, the little fellowships of Anabaptists in southern Germany were victims of ridicule and abuse. Like the American slaves, theirs was a "fellowship of suffering," with one another and with their crucified Lord.

In 1531, Sebastian Franck, a contemporary chronicler, wrote of these Anabaptists: "The Anabaptists spread so rapidly that their teaching soon covered, as it were, the land. They soon gained a large following and baptized many thousands, drawing to themselves many sincere souls who had a zeal for God. For they taught nothing but love, faith, and the cross. . . . They were persecuted with great tyranny, being imprisoned, branded, tortured, and executed by fire, water, and sword. In a few years very many were put to death."

Among those who died was Michael Sattler, a young but respected leader of the movement. He first encountered the evangelical message while serving as prior of the Benedictine monastery of St. Peter's in Breigau, South Germany. Under the influence of William Reublin, an Anabaptist leader in the area, he joined the former followers of the Swiss reformer Ulrich Zwingli. In Zurich they were known as Swiss Brethren. In November 1525, the Zurich authorities struck out against the Anabaptists and banished them from the territory. Sattler fled to Strassburg where he was able to discuss the Anabaptist position with other reformers.

A bit later he assumed missionary work in the region of Württemberg and was so successful that he was chosen to preside over the influential Anabaptist conference at Schleitheim early in 1527. Shortly after this meeting, Austrian authorities arrested him and brought him to trial for heresy.

The account of Sattler's trial and death, along with hundreds of other Anabaptist accounts, was preserved for generations of Mennonites in a volume titled *Martyrs' Mirror*. The trial was convened in Rottenburg on Friday, May 17. The nine charges against Sattler were read and Sattler was granted permission to reply to them. He answered each of them and the town clerk called for a decision from the judges.

WAITING ON GOD

The judge asked Michael Sattler whether he too committed it to the court. He replied: "Ministers of God, I am not sent to judge the Word of God. We are sent to testify and hence cannot consent to any adjudication, since we have no command from God concerning it. But we are not for that reason removed from being judged and we are ready to suffer and to await what God is planning to do with us. We will continue in our faith in Christ so long as we have breath in us, unless we be dissuaded from it by the Scriptures."

The town clerk said: "The hangman will instruct you, he will dispute with you, archheretic."

Michael: "I appeal to the Scriptures."

Then the judges arose and went into another room where they remained for an hour and a half and determined on the sentence. In the meantime some [of the soldiers] in the room treated Michael Sattler most unmercifully, heaping reproach upon him. One of them said: "What have you in prospect for yourself and the others that you have so seduced them?" With this he drew a sword which lay upon the table, saying: "See, with this they will dispute with you." But Michael did not answer upon a single word concerning himself but willingly endured it all. One of the prisoners said: "We must not cast pearls before swine." Being also asked why he had not remained a lord [or prior] in the convent, Michael answered: "According to the flesh I was a lord, but it is better as it is."

The judges having returned to the room, the sentence was read. It was as follows: "In the case of the attorney of His Imperial Majesty vs. Michael Sattler, judgment is passed that Michael Sattler shall be delivered to the executioner, who shall lead him to the place of execution and cut out his tongue, then forge him fast to the wagon and thereon with red-hot tongs twice tear pieces from his body; and after he has been brought outside the gate, he shall be plied five times more in the same manner. . . ."

After this had been done in the manner prescribed, he was burned to ashes as a heretic.[14]

15

Signs of Saving Grace

JOHN CALVIN (1509–1564)

What are the sure signs of a genuine Christian? Are there any absolute guarantees that a person has received the life of God?

Over the centuries such questions have troubled Christians. Those, like the Calvinists, who have stressed the grace of God and man's total inability to do anything to gain God's favor have often struggled with the problem of hypocrisy. They have met those who argue, "Since I can do nothing to gain God's love, as you say, I am under no obligation to change my life. It really doesn't matter how I live, God's love is unconditional."

Evidently even John Calvin met those who professed faith in Christ but showed no signs of possessing the grace of God. At least his writings would lead us to believe that he too faced the problem that we might label "cheap grace" or "easy believism."

Calvin came from a small town sixty miles northeast of Paris. He entered the University of Paris at fourteen and mastered not only a brilliant writing style but a skill in logical argument. He left the university in 1528 with his Master of Arts degree. After his father died in 1531, Calvin returned to the university to pursue his interest in the ancient classics. His studies brought him into touch with Protestant ideas circulating in Paris, and a short time later he had what he called an "unexpected conversion."

By late 1533, Calvin was so closely linked with Protestant views that he was forced to flee Paris. He found refuge in Basel, where he published his first edition of his highly influential *Institutes of the Christian Religion*. The work was so well argued that it gave him European fame almost overnight. A few months later, when he intended to pass through Geneva for quiet study at Strassburg, he met the reformer William Farel, who insisted that he stay in Geneva and assume leadership of the reformation in the city. For the next thirty years, Calvin provided spiritual leadership for the bustling city.

Today, Christians who have heard of John Calvin think of him as a theologian. He was one of the giants. But he was also, during all those years at Geneva, a pastor and spiritual guide. This excerpt about the pursuit of holiness is Ford Lewis Battle's attempt to reflect Calvin's own poetic expression of the Christian life.

THE JOURNEY'S FEEBLE PACE

Here I must address my words to those
Who of Christ have naught but title,
Yet wish to be considered Christians.
How shameless indeed are they to boast
About His sacred name
When no one has anything to do with Him
Save one who by the gospel word
Knows Him in truth!
But St. Paul denies any man has received
True knowledge of Him
Save him who has set out
"To put off the old man corrupt
In disordered desires," to be clad
With Christ. . . .
No doctrine of tongue the gospel is,
But of life itself;
Not to be grasped in understanding and memory only
As other disciplines are, it must
Entirely grip the soul;
Must have its seat and dwelling
Deep in the heart—
Else it has not been in truth received.
Well, then, let them stop boasting
Of what they're not,
Or show themselves disciples
Of the Christ. . . .

I do not require that the morals of the Christian man
Be pure and perfect gospel (although
Such consummation is to be desired
And striven for).
No, I do not require so strictly,
So rigorously, a Christian perfection
That I would recognize as Christian
Only him who has attained it.
For thus measured, all human beings
Would be excluded from the church,
Since one will not find any of them
Not still removed.
Although he has profited greatly,
The majority has still scarcely advanced at all.

What then? We must surely have this end
Before our eyes to which every act

76

Is aimed: to strive toward the perfection
The Lord requires of us. Necessary it is,
I say, to strive and to aspire to reach it. . . .
But while we dwell
in this earthly prison, none of us
Is strong and determined enough to hasten
On this path with the eagerness he ought;
In fact the greater part of us is so weak and feeble
As to waver and limp and be unable
Much to advance.

So let us each go at his feeble pace,
Not ceasing to pursue the journey once begun.
None will so feebly journey as not to advance
Some little daily, to reach his homeland.
Let us then not cease to strive thither
That we progress unceasingly
In the Lord's way.
Let us not lose courage even though
Our progress is but slight.
For even though the actuality may not correspond
To our desire, when today outstrips
Yesterday, all is not lost.
Only let us look with pure and true simplicity
Toward the goal; let us strive
To reach our end, not fondly puffing up ourselves
With vain adulation, not excusing our vices.
Let us strive unceasingly to make
Ourselves become from day to day
Better than we are, until we reach
The sovran goodness, which throughout our lives
We've sought and followed, to grasp it
When, freed from the weakness of our flesh,
We shall become full participants in it,
When God receives us into His fellowship.[15]

16

True Worship

JOHANN ARNDT (1555–1621)

Religion, including the Christian faith, is always in danger of ossification, of substituting the dead letter for the life-giving spirit, of confidence in creed and ritual rather than in the power of the living God. The experience is as near as the next worship service in our own local church.

In the first half of the sixteenth century, the Protestant Reformers were moved by Martin Luther's bold, new doctrine of justification through faith alone. They dared to cry out against the lifeless formalism of the Church of Rome: selfish monks, masses for the dead, worldly popes. And, in time, changes came: educated pastors, translations of the Bible, evangelical catechisms, congregational hymns, and understandable sermons.

By the end of the same century, however, the Reformation was in dire need of reform. In large sections of Germany, orthodox Lutheran pastors simply replaced orthodox Catholic priests. The passion for security and status knows no denominational boundaries.

Scholars call Johann Arndt "the hidden and powerful source" of German pietism. He saw clearly that Martin Luther was far more than an "orthodox theologian." He was also a spiritual guide and advocate of heart-felt faith.

Arndt's early education led him, at twenty-two years of age, to the University at Helmstadt to study medicine. Illness, however, forced him to give up his plans for a medical career. He turned to theology and especially certain mystical authors. His new studies took him to Wittenberg, Strassburg, and Basel. Then in 1584, he became a pastor in Badenborn. After a conflict with his duke, who wanted him to abandon his practice of exorcism before baptism, he moved in 1599 to Braunschweig. He found the city engaged in a struggle with the duke and the spiritual life of the community extremely low. Under these conditions, Arndt wrote *True Christianity*. He explained, in his preface, why he wrote the book. Many people were praising God verbally while living ungodly lives. The book is part protest and part program.

In this excerpt from *True Christianity*, Arndt shows that formal worship consisting of orthodox creeds, official clergymen, and precise ritual may be a religious corpse, which lacks all the vital signs of true worship of the heart.

THE PROPER FIRE

The sons of Aaron offered unholy fire before the Lord and fire came forth from the presence of the Lord and devoured them (Leviticus 10:1–2).

The unholy fire signifies false worship, for it was not of that fire which continually burned before the altar, which God had commanded to be used to burn the sacrifice. Since the sons of Aaron acted against God's commandments, God punished them with the fire of vengeance, which consumed them. . . .

If we wish to understand properly what true worship is, we must set the Old and the New Testament against one another and discover what it is in the comparison or collation. The external worship of the Old Testament offered image and witness of the Messiah in the external ceremonies that had to be established according to the clear letter of the Law. In these marvelous images and figures, faithful Jews saw from afar the Messiah, believed in him, and were made holy through him by the promise. Our worship in the New Testament is no longer external, in typological ceremonies, rubrics, and commandments, but is internal in spirit and in truth, that is in the faith of a Christian, because through faith the whole moral and ceremonial law is filled, the temple, altar, sacrifice, seat of grace, and priesthood. . . .

Three things belong to true, spiritual, inner, and Christian worship: first, true knowledge of God; second, true knowledge of sin and repentance; third, knowledge of grace and the forgiveness of sins. . . .

The knowledge of God consists in faith that grasps Christ and knows God, God's power, God's love and mercy, God's righteousness, truth, and wisdom, . . .

This is the knowledge of God. It consists in faith and not in an empty knowledge but in a joyous, happy, and living trust, by which I discover in myself, in a strong and consoling way, God's power, how he holds me and bears me, . . .

If one knows and feels the power of God truly in his heart, humility follows, so that he humbles himself before the mighty hand of God. If he knows and senses God's mercy properly, love for neighbor follows. No one can be merciful who has not understood God's mercy. . . .

This is the true knowledge of God in which repentance consists, and repentance consists in a change of mind and the renewal of the mind for the improvement of life. This is the other aspect of inner, true worship and it is the proper fire that man is to bring to the sacrifice. Without it, the wrath of God and the fire of vengeance will come over us.

Priests were not to drink wine or strong drink when they went into the tabernacle (Leviticus 10:9). This signifies that if a man wishes to go into the eternal tabernacle of God, that is, to eternal life, he must give up the pleasure and lusts of the flesh of this world and everything by which the flesh conquers the spirit, so that the flesh will not be stronger than the spirit and conquer it. . . .

The third aspect of true, inner, spiritual, proper worship is the forgiveness of sins. It flows from repentance as repentance flows from the true knowledge of God. These are three but are one in truth, for this is the one true knowledge of God. . . .

Note that Moses' law is now given in spirit and is changed into an inner, holy, new life and Moses' sacrifice is changed into the true repentance by which we offer to God our bodies and souls and bring to him a needful thank offering and give to him alone the honor, . . . that his grace might be properly praised and honored with a thankful heart and voice into eternity.[16]

17

The Transforming Life

TERESA OF AVILA (1515–1582)

T he recent drug epidemic in North America and Western Europe has raised afresh all the old questions about mystical experiences, about consciousness beyond all consciousness. With every painful news story, we are becoming increasingly aware of the deadly power of these mind-altering chemicals.

Christians, therefore, are likely to find any comparison of drugs and prayer a shocking and repulsive idea. When we read the descriptions of prayer from some of the Christian "mystics," however, the parallel virtually jumps out of the pages of the text and lands in the mind of the contemporary reader.

Most Christians in Europe and North America today have been trained to hold all thoughts of mysticism at arms length. That is probably the safest course open to us in a society pervaded by appeals to try this or that "mind-blowing" experience.

Many times in the past, however, Christians have had no such resistance to mystical experiences. Spanish society in the sixteenth century was one of those times. And among the great Catholic mystics of that age, none was greater than Teresa of Avila.

Teresa was a member of a prestigious Spanish family living in Avila, on the Castilian plateau. During her childhood, however, she lost her mother and turned to the Virgin Mary and to books describing the lives of the saints. When she was sixteen, her father sent her away to a boarding school for about eighteen months. Years of ill health followed. But during these same years Teresa discovered her religious calling. In 1536, she left home to enter the Convent of the Incarnation and become a Carmelite nun.

In the 1540s, she confessed to several years of spiritual apathy, even after a miraculous cure of her serious illnesses. In the early 1550s, however, she had a life-changing vision of the suffering Christ and confessed her sins to a Jesuit priest, Father Juan de Padranos. This marked the beginning of her mystical experiences with God.

Now aware of the spiritual laxity in her own convent, Teresa felt compelled by God to found a series of seventeen Carmelite convents, all under the strict discipline of the reformed movement in the order. This zeal made her the target of vicious criticism, but Teresa continued her work and wrote of her life with God, especially her experiences in life-transforming prayer.

In her most extended analysis of prayer, a work called *The Interior Castle*, Teresa draws distinctions that most modern Christians find hard to follow, but one illustration from the life of the silkworm is unusually helpful.

THE PARABLE OF THE SILKWORM

You must have already heard about His marvels manifested in the way silk originates, for only He could have invented something like that. The silkworms come from seeds about the size of little grains of pepper. . . . When the warm weather comes and the leaves begin to appear on the mulberry tree, the seeds start to live, for they are dead until then. The worms nourish themselves on the mulberry leaves until, having grown to full size, they settle on some twigs. There with their little mouths they themselves go about spinning the silk and making some very thick little cocoons in which they enclose themselves. The silkworm, which is fat and ugly, then dies, and a little white butterfly, which is very pretty, comes forth from the cocoon. Now if this were not seen but recounted to us as having happened in other times, who would believe it? Or what reasonings could make us conclude that a thing as nonrational as a worm or a bee could be so diligent in working for our benefit and with so much industriousness. And the poor little worm loses its life in the challenge. This is enough, Sisters, for a period of meditation even though I may say no more to you; in it you can consider the wonders and the wisdom of God. . . .

This silkworm, then, starts to live when by the heat of the Holy Spirit it begins to benefit through the general help given to us all by God and through the remedies left by Him to His Church, by going to confession, reading good books, and hearing sermons, which are the remedies that a soul, dead in its carelessness and sin and placed in the midst of occasions, can make use of. It then begins to live and sustain itself by these things, and by good meditations, until it is grown. Its being grown is what is relevant to what I am saying, for these other things have little importance here.

Well once this silkworm is grown . . . it begins to spin the silk and build the house wherein it will die. I would like to point out here that this house is Christ. Somewhere, it seems to me, I have read or heard that our life is hidden in Christ. . . .

Therefore, courage, my daughters! Let's be quick to do this work and weave this little cocoon by taking away our self-love and self-will, our attachment to any earthly thing, and by performing deeds of penance, prayer, mortification, obedience, and all the other things you know. . . . Let it die; let this silkworm die, as it does in completing what it was created to do! . . .

Now, then, let's see what this silkworm does, for that's the reason I've said everything else. When the soul is, in this prayer, truly dead to the world, a little white butterfly comes forth. O greatness of God! How transformed the soul is when it comes out of this prayer after having been placed within the greatness of God and so closely joined to Him for a little while—in my opinion the union never lasts for as much as a half hour. Truly, I tell you that the soul doesn't recognize itself. Look at the difference there is between an ugly worm and a little white butterfly; that's what the difference is here. . . . It sees within itself a desire to praise the Lord; it would want to dissolve and die a thousand deaths for Him. It soon begins to experience a desire to suffer great trials without its being able to do otherwise. . . .

Oh, now, to see the restlessness of this little butterfly, even though it has never been quieter and calmer in its life, is something to praise God for. And the difficulty is that it doesn't know where to alight and rest. Since it has experienced such wonderful rest, all that it sees on earth displeases it, . . . It no longer has any esteem for the works it did while a worm, . . . it now has wings. How can it be happy walking step by step when it can fly?

Well then, where will the poor little thing go? . . . O Lord, what new trials begin for this soul![17]

18

Discovering God's Presence

FRANCIS OF SALES (1567–1622)

Most spiritual counselors speak often of "the presence of God." They describe it in terms of joy, contentment, and peace even in the midst of life's violent storms. But are there any steps that we can take to increase our spiritual awareness of God's nearness? One popular seventeenth-century Roman Catholic counselor, Francis of Sales, says yes.

Francis was one of the most popular preachers of his day, but we remember him as he wanted to be remembered, as a "director of souls." During the last twenty years of his life, he was the Bishop of Geneva, a spiritual guide for Roman Catholics in the shadows of John Calvin's memory.

Francis' preaching often led people to seek his spiritual counsel. After a series of sermons at Dijon, France, in 1607, Mme Louise Charmoisy dedicated her life to God and sought Francis' spiritual guidance. The material in *Introduction to the Devout Life* is the substance of his advice to her. She is the Philothea addressed in its pages.

Francis came from a noble family in the castle of Sales, fifty miles southwest of Geneva. At twenty-four, he had his doctorate in law and was admitted to the senate of Savoy. He could look forward to a noble heiress for a wife and a position in government for a career. Francis, however, chose the church. In December, 1593, he was ordained a priest.

He volunteered for ministry near Geneva, where the controversy between Catholics and Protestants was raging. He had hopes of winning the "heretics" by Christian love. After four largely unsuccessful years, he was ready to return to Savoy. In 1598, his superiors chose him as bishop's coadjutor, and in 1602, they appointed him Bishop of Geneva.

The Devout Life covers a wide range of spiritual problems and for this reason many consider it one of the best introductions to the devotional life. Our selection here illustrates Francis' ability to give clear, practical instructions for progress in the spiritual life.

THE PRINCE WHO IS PRESENT

To assist you to place yourself in the presence of God, I propose four principal means which you will be able to use in this beginning.

The first consists in a lively and attentive apprehension of God's absolute presence. That is, that God is in all things and in every place. There is not a place in the world in which He is not most truly present. Just as birds, wherever they fly, always meet with the air, so we, wherever we go, or wherever we are, always find God present.

Everyone knows this truth, but everyone does not fully reflect upon it. Blind men, who do not see a prince who is present among them, behave with respect when they are told of his presence. However, because they do not see him, they easily forget that he is present, and having forgotten it, they still more easily lose their respect for him. Alas, Philothea, we do not see God, who is present with us. Although faith assures us of His presence, yet because we do not behold Him with our eyes, we too often forget Him and behave as though He were very far away from us. Although we all know that He is present in all things, because we do not reflect upon it, we act as if we did not know it. That is why before prayer we must always excite in our souls a lively thought and apprehension of the presence of God. . . .

The second means to place yourself in His sacred presence is to reflect that God is not only in the place in which you are, but that He is, in a most particular manner, in your heart and in the very center of your spirit. This He enlivens and animates by His divine presence, being there as the heart of your heart and as the spirit of your spirit. . . . And as St. Paul says that it is in God "we live, and move, and are." Therefore, in consideration of this truth, excite in your heart a profound reverence towards God, who is there so intimately present.

A third means is to consider our Savior in His humanity looking down from heaven on all mankind, but especially on Christians, who are His children, and more particularly on such as are at prayer, whose actions and behavior He observes. This is by no means a mere imagination, but a very truth. . . .

A fourth method consists in making use of the imagination, by representing to ourselves our Savior in His sacred humanity, as if He were near us, as we sometimes imagine a friend to be present, saying "I imagine that I see him who has done this or that," or "It seems to me that I see him," or something similar. . . .

Hence, you will employ one of these four means of placing yourself in the presence of God before prayer. Do not use them all at once, but one at a time, and that briefly and simply.[18]

19

Patterns of Worship (1549 and after)

THE BOOK OF COMMON PRAYER

O ur debt to those Christians who have passed this way before us was expressed magnificently by one twelfth-century scholar, Peter of Blois, when he wrote, "We are like dwarfs on the shoulders of giants, by whose grace we see farther than they." That is a distinct feeling we get when we use the guide for worship in the Anglican Church.

The *Book of Common Prayer* is, for several reasons, almost unique in devotional literature. Most devotional classics were accidents. They were never intended as guidebooks for a Christian public, but as personal journals or letters of spiritual counsel to some friend.

The *Book Common Prayer,* however, was from the start intended for the religious life of a nation, and it has shaped the life of the English people like no other book except the Bible. Through more than four centuries it has found a place, not only in the Church of England, but in the lives of hosts of readers in other churches.

The first edition of the *Book of Common Prayer,* published in 1549, was largely the work of Archbishop Thomas Cranmer during the days of the English reformation. In spite of his eventual martyrdom under Queen "Bloody" Mary, Cranmer was for most of his adult life more of a scholar than a saint. Saints were hard to identify in the English reformation. But, once in a position to shape the Church of England, Cranmer intended to give to his people those riches of the Christian centuries arising from the Bible.

After Cranmer's execution under the devoutly catholic Queen Mary, the *Book of Common Prayer* underwent several revisions until it was finally approved in 1662 in a form that has remained essentially unchanged up to our own time. While our first impression of the *Book of Common Prayer* may focus on its old-fashioned flavor, our more thoughtful reading will reveal its clarity, beauty, and often nobility. Both its thoughts and its language are based firmly on Scripture. In fact, two-thirds of its contents are actual biblical quotations.

Unlike many other devotional classics, the *Book of Common Prayer* is not designed to nurture an individualistic piety. Its devotional pattern is definitely church-centered. It assumes throughout its pages that the Christian moves toward God, not in lonely isolation but among the people of God.

Since the *Book* is intended for corporate worship in the Anglican Church throughout the church year, individual Christians will have their likes and dislikes about portions of the *Book,* but most widely admired and used are the hundreds of prayers and collects scattered throughout the volume. Non-Anglicans will discover that *collects* are simply brief formal prayers in the service of public worship. We can taste the flavor of this devotional classic in the following selections.

A RIGHTEOUS AND SOBER LIFE

A Collect for Grace

O Lord, our heavenly Father, Almighty and everlasting God, who hast safely brought us to the beginning of this day; defend us in the same with thy mighty power; and grant that this day we fall into no sin, neither run into any kind of danger; but that all our doings, being ordered by thy governances, may be righteous in thy sight; through Jesus Christ our Lord. Amen

Collect for the Second Sunday in Advent

Blessed Lord, who hast caused all holy Scriptures to be written for our learning; grant that we may in such wise hear them, read, mark, learn, and inwardly digest them, that by patience and comfort of thy holy Word, we may embrace, and ever hold fast, the blessed hope of everlasting life, which thou hast given us in our Saviour Jesus Christ. Amen.

Collect for the Nativity of Our Lord

Almighty God, who hast given us thy only-begotten Son to take our nature upon him, and as at this time to be born of a pure virgin; Grant that we being regenerate, and made thy children by adoption and grace, may daily be renewed by thy Holy Spirit; through the same Lord Jesus Christ, who liveth and reigneth with thee and the same Spirit ever, one God, world without end. Amen.

Collect for the Sixth Sunday after the Epiphany

O God, whose blessed Son was manifested that he might destroy the works of the devil, and make us the sons of God, and heirs of eternal life; Grant us, we beseech thee, that, having this hope, we may purify ourselves, even as he is pure; that, when he shall appear again with power and great glory, we may be made like unto him in his eternal and glorious kingdom; where with thee, O Father, and thee, O Holy Ghost, he liveth and reigneth ever, one God, world without end. Amen.

A General Thanksgiving

Almighty God, Father of all mercies, we, thine unworthy servants, do give thee most humble and hearty thanks for all thy goodness and loving-kindness to us, and to all men; we bless thee for our creation, preservation, and all the blessings of this life; but above all, for thine inestimable love in the redemption of the world by our Lord Jesus Christ; for the means of grace, and for the hope of glory. And, we beseech thee, give us that due sense of all thy mercies, that our hearts may be unfeignedly thankful; and that we may show forth thy praise, not only with our lips, but in our lives, by giving up our selves to thy service, and by walking before thee in holiness and righteousness all our days; through Jesus Christ our Lord, to whom, with thee and the Holy Ghost, be all honour and glory, world without end. Amen.[19]

20
Confession of Sin

LANCELOT ANDREWES (1555–1626)

G. K. Chesterton, the British novelist, once said that human depravity is the one Christian doctrine that can be proved. One would think so. Evidence of sin is on every hand: crime, domestic violence, wars, pornography, fraud. Even the denial of sin from unbelieving men and women is itself an evidence of the human tragedy. Obviously, then, Christian spiritual guides must prescribe some antidote to this universal human malady.

Among spiritual counselors few seem to have felt the need for confession of sin quite like Lancelot Andrewes, advisor to British monarchs and translator of the King James Bible. He was part of the Puritan Age, but he had serious reservations about Puritan ambitions.

Andrewes was educated at Pembroke Hall, Cambridge and at the time of his ordination in 1580, he held views similar to the Puritans at Cambridge. During the 1580s, however, he sided with the episcopal leaders in the Church of England. When he was made chaplain to Queen Elizabeth, he became a part of that religious establishment that troubled the Puritans deeply.

Under King James I, Andrewes' reputation as a preacher gained him a bishop's post and his scholarship earned him major responsibilities for the translation of the early books of the Old Testament in the Authorized (KJV) Version of 1611.

Through these years of public life, Andrewes maintained his disciplined practice of private devotion to God. And that private Lancelot Andrewes is who most well-read Christians know because he is the one we meet in his *Private Devotions of Lancelot Andrewes.*

Private Devotions was just what the name suggests. Andrewes never intended the little book for publication. Not until he lay dying in 1626 did he place it in the hands of William Laud, then Bishop of Bath and Wells.

Those who admire beauty, symmetry, and order in their worship will appreciate Lancelot Andrewes. He is a man of seasons, days, and hours. He reflects not only the dignity of the King James Version of the Bible, but his kinship with a host of Christian authors in the past. Throughout his *Devotions,* however, there is an undertone of solemnity, created by his periodic confession of sin.

HEAL MY SOUL!

Meditation

The day is gone,
and I give Thee thanks, O Lord.
Evening is at hand,
make it bright unto us.
As day has its evening
so also has life;
the even of life is age,
age has overtaken me,
make it bright unto us.
Cast me not away in the time of age;
forsake me not when my strength faileth me.
Even to my old age be Thou He,
and even to hoar hairs carry me;
do Thou make, do Thou bear,
do Thou carry and deliver me.
Abide with me, Lord
for it is toward evening,
and the day is far spent
of this fretful life.
Let Thy strength be made perfect
in my weakness.
Day is fled and gone,
life too is going,
this lifeless life.
Night cometh,
and cometh death,
the deathless death.
Near as is the end of day,
so too the end of life:
We then, also remembering it,
beseech of Thee
for the close of our life,
that Thou wouldest direct it in peace,
Christian, acceptable,
sinless, shameless,
and, if it please Thee, painless,
Lord, O Lord,
gathering us together
under the feet of Thine Elect,
when Thou wilt, and as Thou wilt,
only without shame and sins.

Confession

Lord,
as we add day to day
so sin to sin.
The just falleth seven times a day;
and I, an exceeding sinner,
seventy times seven;
wonderful, a horrible thing, O Lord.
But I turn with groans
from my evil ways,
and I return into my heart,
and with all my heart I turn to Thee,
O God of penitents and Saviour of sinners;
and evening by evening I will return
in the innermost marrow of my soul;
and my soul out of the deep
crieth unto Thee.
I have sinned, O Lord, against Thee,
heavily against Thee;
alas, alas, woe is me! for my misery.
I repent, O me! I repent, spare me, O Lord,
I repent, O me, I repent,
help Thou my impenitence.
Be appeased, spare me, O Lord;
be appeased, have mercy on me;
I said, Lord, have mercy upon me,
heal my soul, for I have sinned against
Thee.
Have mercy upon me, O Lord,
after Thy great goodness,
according to the multitude of Thy mercies
do away mine offenses.
Remit the guilt,
heal the wound,
blot out the stains,
clear away the shame,
rescue from the tyranny,
and make me not a public example.
O bring Thou me out of my trouble,
cleanse Thou me from secret fault,
keep back Thy servant also from
presumptuous sins.
My wanderings of mind
and idle talking
lay not to my charge.
Remove the dark and muddy flood
of foul and wicked thoughts.
O Lord,
I have destroyed myself;
whatever I have done amiss, pardon mercifully.[20]

21

A Parson's Prayer

GEORGE HERBERT (1593–1633)

What we think of persons determines what we ask of them. Think of the different ways we approach our father, our senator, and our dentist. To ask great things of someone, we must believe that he has both the power and the will to grant the request.

That is why our prayers are a reflection of our theology. What we think of God determines how we pray. Feeble faith is the father of feeble prayers. Muscular faith produces muscular prayers. We can see this truth demonstrated in the prayers of George Herbert.

Herbert lived during the reign of England's King James I. He was aware of the Puritan objection to many of James' policies but chose to remain in the Church of England. He entered public life as an orator at Cambridge and was on the threshold of a career in the king's service when King James' death, followed by Herbert's own mother's passing, apparently prompted him to enter the ministry. In 1629, he became a country parson at Bemerton, near Salisbury. Like his contemporary and mentor John Donne, he wrote a number of best selling poems. But he was also a caring "shepherd of the flock" at Bemerton.

Herbert wrote *The Country Parson,* his description of a godly minister, for personal reasons. He wanted "a mark to aim at." He made every effort to live up to the image of the ideal parson that he had painted. Only after his death was it published.

The following prayer was the one Herbert's ideal minister offered before preaching.

BEFORE THY FACE

Oh Almighty and everlasting Lord God! Majesty, and Power, and Brightness, and Glory! How shall we dare to appear before thy face, who are contrary to thee, in all we call thee? For we are darkness, and weakness, and filthiness, and shame. Misery and sin fill our days: yet thou art our Creator, and we thy work: Thy hands both made us, and also made us lords of all Thy creatures;

giving us one world in ourselves, and another to serve us: then didst thou place us in Paradise, and wert proceeding still on in thy Favors, until we interrupted thy Counsels, disappointed thy Purposes, and sold our God, our glorious, our gracious God for an apple.

Oh write it! Oh brand it in our foreheads forever: for an apple once we lost our God and still lose him for no more; for money, for meat, for diet: But thou Lord, art patience and pity, and sweetness, and love; therefore we sons of men are not consumed. Thou hast exalted thy mercy above all things; and hast made our salvation, not our punishment, thy glory: so that then where sin abounded, not death, but grace superabounded; accordingly, when we had sinned beyond any help in heaven or earth, then thou saidest, Lo, I come! Then did the Lord of life, unable of himself to die, contrive to do it. He took flesh, he wept, he died; for his enemies he died; even for those that derided him then, and still despise him.

Blessed Savior! many waters could not quench thy love! nor no pit overwhelm it. But though the streams of thy blood were current (or flowing) through darkness, grave, and hell; yet by these thy conflicts, and seemingly hazards, didst thou arise triumphant, and therein mad'st us victorious.

Neither doth thy love yet stay here! for, this word of thy rich peace, and reconciliation, thou has committed, not to Thunder, or Angels, but to silly and sinful men: even to me, pardoning my sins, and bidding me go feed the people of thy love.

Blessed be the God of Heaven and Earth! who only doth wond'rous things. Awake therefore, my Lute, and my Viol! awake all my powers to glorify thee! We praise thee! we bless thee! we magnify thee forever! And now, Oh Lord! in the power of thy Victories, and in the ways of thy Ordinances, and in the Truth of thy Love, Lo, we stand here, beseeching thee to bless thy word, . . . Oh, make it a word of power and peace, to convert those who are not thine, and to confirm those that are. . . . Oh, let not our foolish and unworthy hearts rob us of the continuance of this thy sweet love: but pardon our sins, and perfect what thou hast begun. . . . Oh Lord, hear, Oh Lord forgive! Oh Lord, Hearken, and do so for thy blessed Son's sake.[21]

Part 4

Saints in the Puritan Period

L ife is a journey. That is a distinct impression that many of us have from time to time. "What have I really accomplished?" we ask ourselves. "Where am I headed?" Perhaps the question comes with a flip of the calendar, or the news that a high-school friend has passed away. Whatever the reminder, we follow the thought and soon we find ourselves reflecting on the brevity of life and all that we intended to do—once upon a time.

In his classic allegory *Pilgrim's Progress,* John Bunyan adopts this idea that life is a journey to set forth his Puritan understanding of the Christian life. In the opening scene of his story, the pilgrim is about to undertake his uncertain journey, so Bunyan pictures Christian "standing in a certain place with his face from his own house, a book in his hand and a great burden on his back. As he reads, he weeps and cries, 'What shall I do?' "

The suggestion that life is a winding and treacherous path comes from the Bible itself where men and women of faith are called pilgrims and strangers who "long for another country—a heavenly one" (Hebrews 11:16). The Puritans seized the idea and made it basic to their whole understanding of the Christian life.

In modern times, marked by zeal for individual rights and sexual freedom, "puritan" is an ugly word. It has come to stand for a religious snob, filled with fears of sex, who does his best to keep people from having fun. This negative view of the term seems to have captured popular thinking in a social backlash of Victorian stuffiness. Early in the twentieth century, American journalist H. L. Mencken summed up the popular image in his quip that Puritanism was "the haunting fear that someone, somewhere may be happy."

Anyone who has the slightest appreciation for evangelical Christianity, however, knows that this austere image of a Puritan is little more than a caricature. The original Puritans were anything but straight-laced. They stood for change, a new day in England. Their plans for their country were based upon a deep conviction that spiritual conversion was crucial to Christianity. This rebirth separated the Puritan from the mass of mankind and endowed him with the privileges and the duties of the people of God. The church may prepare a person for this experience and after it the church may guide him in the Christian life, but the heart of the experience, the reception of the grace of God, is beyond the church's control.

THE TIMES

In its crusade to reshape England, the Puritan movement passed through three rather clearly marked periods. First, under Queen Elizabeth I (1558–1603), it tried to "purify" the Church of England along the lines of Calvin's Geneva. Second, under James I and Charles I (1603–1642), it resisted the claims of the monarchy and suffered under royal pressures designed to force conformity to a high-church style Christianity. Third, during England's Civil War and Oliver Cromwell's rule (1642–1660), Puritans had a chance to shape the national church in England but failed, in part, because of their own internal dissensions.

Such an outline suggests, as it should, that Puritanism originally had a public side as well as a personal side. It began with an individual's experience of the redeeming grace of God but moved on to stress the saint's mission in the world, the shaping of society according to biblical principles. In its emphasis upon the interior life of the saint, Puritanism was a major contributor to later evangelical Christianity with its born-again message. In its stress upon a disciplined "nation under God" and his laws, it contributed significantly to the national character of the American people.

As a result of the English Civil War and the execution of King Charles I in 1649, Puritanism was discredited in the eyes of many Englishmen. By the end of the seventeenth century, the movement as a political force was pretty well spent. What remained was Puritanism as a spiritual power.

Puritan spirituality started with the Protestant emphasis on justification by faith alone. A true Christian is justified by faith and therefore fully in a "state of grace." Puritans, however, believed firmly that this justification was more than a doctrine. It was the basis of all spiritual life. Spirituality was not a means of achieving some spiritual state. It was the lively expression of a relationship already secure in God.

In his treatise *A Garden of Spiritual Flowers,* Puritan leader Richard Rogers (1550?–1618) indicates, in rather typical fashion, that life's journey toward "true happiness" passes through three "parts." The first part deals with the misery of sin; the second part, with the peace that comes from the deliverance from sin; and the third part, with how to "change thy life, and conform it unto the will of God, and gives thee direction how to walk with God daily."

Here we have the Puritan counterpart of the three stages of monastic perfection: self-denial, the cultivation of virtues, and the love of God. In Puritan thinking, it is genuine repentance, heartfelt forgiveness and deliverance, and personal holiness to the glory of God.

A few other spiritual guides included in Part 4 make clear that Puritans were not the only Christians in the seventeenth century concerned about the spiritual life. Anglicans and Roman Catholics had their own advocates for a personal experience of the grace of God.

22

The Power of Choice

BLAISE PASCAL (1623–1662)

Do not wonder," wrote a seventeenth-century saint, "to see simple people believe without reasoning. God imparts to them love of Him and hatred of self. He inclines their heart to believe. Men will never believe with a saving and real faith, unless God inclines their heart; and they will believe as soon as He inclines it."

The words of John Calvin? No, the convictions of a scientific genius, a Roman Catholic—Blaise Pascal. They are a reminder that devotion to God in the "Puritan Period" was no Puritan monopoly. Christians from several traditions dared to announce their personal faith even as influential voices were questioning the possibility.

During the seventeenth century, the cluster of assumptions about reality that we often call "the Enlightenment" began to displace Christianity in the hearts and minds of many Western people. It made faith even more difficult because modern men and women developed an inordinate confidence in human reason and looked for the happiness promised to those who followed its laws. In many people's minds, science, with all its products, simply made God obsolete. How do we find faith in our technological age?

One of the first Christians to struggle with that question was a pioneer in modern science. Blaise Pascal's name lives today in a computer language named after him, which is appropriate because he designed the first mechanical computer. He also used a set of dice to work out the theory of probability. And in physics he discovered the principle of hydraulics that we call Pascal's law.

Pascal was also, along with his sister, a member of the Jansenist movement seeking reform in the French Catholic Church. He wrote a series of brilliant essays titled *The Provincial Letters* in which he defended Jansenist views and attacked the practices of the Jesuits. After his death friends found among his papers twenty-seven bundles of notes for a major book he had planned, which defended Christianity against the growing rationalism of his time. Today we call these Pascal's *Pensèes (Thoughts)*. They have become classics of thoughtful Christian devotion.

Pascal dared to challenge the sovereignty of reason. "The heart has its reason," he wrote, "which reason does not know." And he underscored the limitations of reason because he knew that man could find neither God nor happiness by reason alone. "It is the heart which experiences God, and not the reason. This, then, is faith: God felt by the heart, not by the reason." That is the sort of statement that has made Pascal a favorite among students of the devotional classics. Here are a few lines from his pen that stress the importance of personal commitment.

FAITH'S WAGER

The will is one of the chief factors in belief, not that it creates belief, but because things are true or false according to the aspect in which we look at them. The will, which prefers one aspect to another, turns away the mind from considering the qualities of all that it does not like to see; and thus the mind, moving according to the will, stops to consider the aspect which it likes, and so judges by what it sees. . . .

"God is, or He is not." But to which side shall we incline? Reason can decide nothing here. . . . A game is being played at the extremity of this infinite distance where heads or tails will turn up. What will you wager? According to reason, you can do neither the one thing nor the other; according to reason, you can defend neither of the propositions.

Do not then reprove for error those who have made a choice; for you know nothing about it. "No, but I blame them for having made, not this choice; for again both he who chooses heads and he who chooses tails are equally at fault, they are both wrong. The true course is not to wager at all."

Yes; but you must wager. It is not optional. You are embarked. Which will you choose then? Let us see. Since you must choose, let us see which interests you least. You have two things to lose, the true and the good; and two things at stake, your reason and your will, your knowledge and your happiness; and your nature has two things to shun error and misery. Your reason is not more shocked in choosing one rather than the other, since you must of necessity choose. This is one point settled. But your happiness? Let us weigh the gain and the loss in wagering that God is. Let us estimate these two chances. If you gain, you gain all; if you lose, you lose nothing. Wager, then, without hesitation that He is. . . .

What harm will befall you in taking this side? You will be faithful, honest, humble, grateful, generous, a sincere friend, truthful. Certainly you will not have those poisonous pleasures, glory and luxury; but will you not have others? I will tell you that you will thereby gain in this life, and that, at each step you take on this road, you will see so great certainty of gain, so much nothingness in what you risk, that you will at last recognize that you have wagered for something certain and infinite, for which you have given nothing.

The God of Christians is not a God who is simply the author of mathematical truths, or of the order of the elements; that is the view of heathen and Epicureans. He is not merely a God who exercises providence over the life and fortunes of men, to bestow on those who worship Him a long and happy life. . . .

The God of Christians is a God of love and of comfort, a God who fills the soul and heart of those whom He possesses, a God who makes them conscious of their inward wretchedness, and His infinite mercy, who unites Himself to their inmost soul, who fills it with humility and joy, with confidence and love, who renders them incapable of any other end than Himself.[22]

$$23$$

Christian Humility

JEREMY TAYLOR (1613–1667)

For a generation now, powerful invisible forces in Western societies have encouraged personal choices and self-interest. Ours, we know, is the "me generation." Selfishness is in style. Messages in the media tell us that our first and last thought ought to be "What's in it for me?" We are supposed to value self-worth, self-esteem, and self-expression.

In such a climate, Christians should experience few emotional shocks when rock stars and television personalities ridicule and reject Christian values and virtues. Many of today's images of pleasure and success simply contradict the personal qualities of the Lord Jesus Christ. Perhaps the clearest evidence of this clash in values appears in that traditional Christian virtue we call "humility."

Humility, as we have seen, was one of the preeminent virtues for the medieval monks. It was almost synonymous with Christlikeness. But the monks were not the only spiritual guides to sing the praises of humility. The best example of this admiration outside monasticism is probably found in the writings of Jeremy Taylor.

Taylor was born at Cambridge, England, and found it only natural to attend the university in his hometown. His gift of eloquence soon made him a prominent public figure. The Archbishop of Canterbury, William Laud, nominated Taylor as his chaplain.

When the English Civil War broke out in the 1640s, Taylor, like his contemporaries Baxter and Bunyan, was forced to declare his loyalties. He chose to be loyal to the king. This meant that when the royal cause collapsed and Oliver Cromwell seized power, Taylor was forced out of public life and into a less conspicuous ministry at Charmarthenshire. These years were his productive writing years. He penned his two best known works during these years, *Holy Living* in 1650 and *Holy Dying* in 1651.

When Charles II restored the monarchy in 1660, English church authorities rewarded Taylor's loyalty to the crown by appointing him Bishop of Down and Conner. Most Christians, however, know little of Taylor's life. If they have met him at all, they have probably done so through his baroque prose in *Holy Living* or *Holy Dying*. Here is Taylor's recommendation of Christian humility.

THE VAST DESCENT

Humility is the great ornament and jewel of the Christian religion, . . . first put into a discipline and made a part of a religion by our Lord Jesus Christ, . . .

For all the world, all that we are, and all that we have, our bodies and our souls, our actions and our sufferings, our conditions at home, our accidents [or experiences] abroad, our many sins and our seldom virtues, are as so many arguments to make our souls dwell low in the deep valleys of humility. . . .

The humble man . . . does not . . . pursue the choice of his own will, but in all things lets God choose for him and his superiors in those things which concern them. He does not murmur against commands. . . . He patiently bears injuries. He is always unsatisfied in his own conduct, resolutions, and counsels. He is a great lover of good men, and praiser of wise men, and a censurer of no man. He is modest in his speech, and reserved in his laughter. He fears when he hears himself commended, lest God make another judgment concerning his actions than men do. . . . He mends his faults, and gives thanks, when he is admonished.

The grace of humility is exercised by these following rules:

Love to be concealed, and little esteemed: be content to want [or lack] praise, never being troubled when thou art slighted or undervalued; for thou canst not undervalue thyself, and if thou thinkest so meanly as there is reason, no contempt will seem unreasonable, and therefore it will be very tolerable.

Never speak anything directly to thy praise or glory; that is, with purpose to be commended, and for no other end.

When thou hast said or done a thing for which thou receivest praise or estimation, take it indifferently, and return it to God, reflecting upon him as the giver of the gift, or the blesser of the action, . . . and give God thanks for making thee an instrument of his glory, for the benefit of others.

Secure a good name to thyself by living virtuously and humbly; but let this good name be nursed abroad, and never be brought home to look upon it. . . .

Use no stratagems and devices to get praise. Some use to inquire into the faults of their own actions or discourses on purpose to hear that it was well done or spoken and without fault. . . .

Suffer [or permit] others to be praised in thy presence, and entertain their good and glory with delight; but at no hand disparage them, or lessen the report, or make an objection; and think not the advancement of thy brother is a lessening of thy worth. . . .

Never compare thyself with others, unless it be to advance them and to depress thyself. . . .

Remember that the blessed Saviour of the world hath done more to prescribe, and transmit, and secure this grace, than any other; his whole life being a great continued example of humility, a vast descent from the glorious bosom of His Father, to the womb of a poor maiden, to the form of a servant, to the miseries of a sinner, to a life of labor, to a state of poverty, to a death of malefactors, to the grave of death, and to the intolerable calamities which we deserved; . . .[23]

24

Christin the Heart

HENRY SCOUGAL (1650–1678)

P erhaps the best-known and most-admired saint in our time is Mother
Teresa of Calcutta. Malcolm Muggeridge, in his *Something Beautiful
for God,* reveals a precious part of the Nobel Prize winner's secret. "We need
to find God," she says, "and he cannot be found in noise and restlessness.
God is the friend of silence. See how nature—trees, flowers, grass—grow in
silence; see the stars, the moon and sun, how they move in silence. . . . The
more we receive in silent prayer, the more we can give in our active life. We
need silence to be able to touch souls. The essential thing is not what we say,
but what God says to us and through us."

Three centuries ago Henry Scougal made the same point during his brief
lifetime. He lived only twenty-eight years. Yet students of the classics call him
"Aberdeen's immortal mystic." His *The Life of God in the Soul of Man* may
be the finest devotional classic to come out of Scotland.

Born June, 1650, in Fifeshire, Scotland, Scougal became something of a
child prodigy. At fourteen he entered King's College, Aberdeen, where his
father was chancellor. Four years later he received his Master of Arts degree.
During these college days, he led a student devotional society similar to the
Holy Club that John and Charles Wesley would later lead at Oxford.

Only a year after securing his masters degree, Scougal became a professor
of philosophy, a position he held for three years. In 1673, at twenty-four years
of age, he accepted a pastoral position in Aberdeenshire but left it a year later
when his church synod unanimously elected him Professor of Divinity at
King's College. Here at Aberdeen he spent the last three years of his short life
lecturing and writing. He died on June 13, 1678, a victim of tuberculosis.

Today on the north side of the chapel at King's College, a tablet of black
marble recalls his memory. But Scougal's influence lived on in his books,
especially *The Life of God in the Soul of Man.* The impact upon the Wesleyan
Revival was direct and deep. John Wesley's mother, Susanna, found it "an
excellent good book." Later, George Whitefield, the incendiary evangelist of
the American Great Awakening, remarked, "I never knew what true religion
was till God sent me that excellent treatise by the hand of my never-to-be-

forgotten friend.'' That friend was Charles Wesley, whose brother John edited and abridged *The Life of God in the Soul of Man* in 1742.

In spite of the fact that Scougal originally intended *The Life of God in the Soul of Man* as a letter of spiritual direction for a friend, the "letter" of twenty thousand words came to the attention of Bishop Gilbert Burnet, who published it. It found immediate popularity as a devotional classic. In this brief excerpt we find the heart of Scougal's counsel.

THE SCALES OF A BALANCE

True religion is a union of the soul with God, a real participation of the divine nature, the very image of God drawn upon the soul, or, in the apostle's phrase, it is Christ formed within us. . . . The root of the divine life is faith; the chief branches are love to God, charity to man, purity, and humility. . . . Faith has the same place in the divine life which sense has in the natural, being indeed nothing else but a kind of sense or feeling persuasion of spiritual things: it extends itself into all divine truths; but in our lapsed estate it has a peculiar relation to the declarations of God's mercy and reconcilableness to sinners through a Mediator, . . .

The love of God is a delightful and affectionate sense of the divine perfections which makes the soul resign and sacrifice itself wholly unto him, desiring above all things to please him, and delighting in nothing so much as in fellowship and communion with him, and being ready to do or suffer anything for his sake or his pleasure. . . .

But . . . if we desire to have our souls molded to this holy frame, to become partakers of the divine nature, and have Christ formed in our hearts, we must seriously resolve, . . . to avoid and abandon all sinful practices. There can be no treaty of peace till once we lay down these weapons of rebellion wherewith we fight against heaven. . . . Every wilful sin gives a mortal wound to the soul, and puts it at a greater distance from God and goodness; and we can never hope to have our hearts purified from corrupt affections, unless we cleanse our hands from vicious actions. . . .

Let us consider ourselves under the all-seeing eye of that divine majesty as in the midst of an infinite globe of light, which compasseth us about both behind and before, and pierceth to the innermost corners of our soul. The sense and remembrance of the divine presence is the most ready and effectual means, both to discover what is unlawful, and restrain us from it. . . .

Our next essay [endeavor] must be to wean our affections from created things, and all the delights and entertainments of the lower life, . . . and this we must do by possessing our minds with a deep persuasion of the vanity and emptiness of worldly enjoyments. This is an ordinary theme, and everybody can make declamations upon it; but . . . how few understand and believe what they say! These notions float in our brains, and come sliding from our tongues, but we have no deep impression of them in our spirits; we feel not the truth which we pretend to believe. . . .

The soul of man is a vigorous and active nature, and hath in it a raging and unextinguishable thirst, an immaterial kind of fire, always catching at some object or other, in conjunction wherewith it thinks to be happy; . . . The love of the world and the love of God are like the scales of a balance! As one falleth, the other doth rise. . . . It doth, therefore, nearly concern us, to convince ourselves of the emptiness and vanity of creature-enjoyments, . . . Can . . . the esteem and affection of silly creatures, like myself, satisfy a rational and immortal soul? . . .

When we have got our corruptions restrained, and our natural appetites . . . in some measure subdued, we must proceed to such exercises as have a more immediate tendency to excite and awaken the divine life. . . .

Let us be often lifting up our hearts toward God; and if we do not say that we love him above all things, let us, at least, acknowledge that it is our duty, . . . and so do it. . . .

He hath placed us in a rich and well-furnished world, and liberally provided for all our necessities; . . . he hath long contended with a stubborn world, and thrown down many a blessing upon them; and when all his other gifts could not prevail, he at last made a gift of himself, to testify his affection and engage theirs. The account which we have of our Savior's life in the gospel doth all along present us with the story of his love; all the pains that he took, and the troubles that he endured, were the wonderful effects and uncontrollable evidence of it . . . God . . . did not account the blood of his Son too great a price for their redemption.[24]

25

Preparing for Death

JOHN BUNYAN (1628–1688)

T he statistics on death," George Bernard Shaw, the British novelist, once said, "are quite impressive." The reason, says Christianity, lies in the nature of death. It is a consequence of sin, that universal human propensity to self-destruct. If death, then, is a dreadful certainty, how shall we prepare for it?

Three-and-a-half centuries ago, a poor handyman in England painted a memorable picture of life's journey and included a striking perspective on the Christian view of "death."

He began his story, "As I walked through the wilderness of this world, I lighted on a certain place, where was a den; and I laid me down in that place to sleep: and as I slept I dreamed a dream." The "den" was a jail in Bedford, England, where John Bunyan was imprisoned as an unlicensed Baptist preacher. The "dream," it turns out, was his *Pilgrim's Progress,* the classic allegory of Christian's journey from the City of Destruction to the Celestial City.

Someone has said that for two centuries most homes in England had two books if no others—the King James Bible and *Pilgrim's Progress.* When we read the sermons of Charles Haddon Spurgeon, preached just a century ago, we discover that he assumed his congregation's knowledge of Bunyan's characters. Today is quite another matter. Even many well-read Christians have totally ignored *Pilgrim's Progress.*

We can trace this shift in popularity to the difficulty in finding an edition of the work that retains Bunyan's original feel for common speech and to the widespread rejection today of Bunyan's Puritan theology. In spite of this decline in popularity, however, *Pilgrim's Progress* justly deserves the title "classic."

According to his own testimony, as a youth Bunyan had "few equals . . . both for cursing, swearing, lying, and blaspheming the holy name of God." He was a poor tinker (or general repairman) who married an equally poor woman. His wife brought to the marriage, however, two religious books that launched Bunyan's search for God. Like Luther, after a time of torment and doubt,

Bunyan experienced the forgiveness of God. Almost at once, he plunged into preaching the grace of God.

With the demise of Cromwell's Puritan-led Republic and the restoration of the English monarchy in 1660, Bunyan's refusal to conform to Anglican policies led to his twelve-year imprisonment, when he wrote *Pilgrim's Progress*. After his release from prison in 1672 he continued preaching until he caught pneumonia while on a pastoral call to reconcile a father and his son.

Here is Bunyan's description of the Christian preparation and experience of death.

NO OTHER PLAN

Now I saw in my dream that the highway up which Christian was to go was fenced on either side with a wall, and that wall is called Salvation. Up this way therefore did burdened Christian run, but not without great difficulty because of the load on his back.

He ran thus till he came at a place somewhat ascending; and upon that place stood a Cross, and a little below in the bottom, a Sepulchre. So I saw in my dream that just as Christian came up to the Cross, his burden loosed from off his shoulders and fell from off his back; and began to tumble, and so continued to do till it came to the mouth of the Sepulchre, where it fell in, and I saw it no more.

Then Christian was glad and lightsome, and said with a merry heart, He has given me rest by his sorrow, and life by his death. Then he stood still a while to look and wonder; for it was very surprising to him that the sight of the Cross should thus ease him of his burden. He looked therefore, and looked again, even till the springs that were in his head sent the waters down his cheeks.

Now, as he stood looking and weeping, behold three Shining Ones came to him and saluted him with "Peace be to thee." So the first said to him, "Thy sins be forgiven": the second stripped him of his rags and clothed him with a change of raiment; the third also set a mark on his forehead and gave him a roll with a seal upon it, which he bid him look on as he ran, and that he should give it in at the Celestial Gate; so they went their way. Then, Christian leaped three times for joy and went on singing.

So I saw that when they [Christian and Hopeful] awoke, they addressed themselves to go up to the city. But . . . the reflection of the sun upon the city . . . was so extremely glorious that they could not, as yet, with open face behold it, . . . So I saw that as they went on, there met them two men in raiment that shone like gold, also their faces shone as the light.

These men asked the pilgrims whence they came; and they told them. . . . Then said the men that met them, You have but two difficulties more to meet with, and you are in the city.

Christian then and his companion asked the men to go along with them, so they told them they would. . . .

Now I further saw that betwixt them and the gate was a river, but there was no bridge to go over; the river was very deep. . . . The pilgrims then, especially Christian, began to despond in their minds and looked this way and that, but no way could be found by them by which they might escape the river. Then they asked the men if the waters were all of a depth. They said, No; yet they could not help them in that case; for, said they, You shall find it deeper or shallower, as you believe in the King of the place.

They addressed themselves to the water; and entering, Christian began to sink, and, crying out to his good friend Hopeful, he said, I sink in deep waters; the billows go over my head, all his waves go over me! . . .

Then said the other, Be of good cheer, my brother; I feel the bottom, and it is good. Then said Christian, Ah, my friend, the sorrows of death have compassed me about; I shall not see the land that flows with milk and honey. . . . Then said Hopeful, . . . These troubles and distresses that you go through in these waters are no sign that God hath forsaken you; but are sent to try you whether you will call to mind that which heretofore you have received of his goodness, and live upon him in your distresses. . . . And with that Christian broke out with a loud voice, Oh, I see him again! and he tells me, "When thou passest through the waters, I will be with thee; . . ."

Then they both took courage, and the enemy was after that as still as a stone until they were gone over.[25]

26

Self-Denial

JOHN FLAVEL (1630–1691)

I n an affluent society, justification of self-indulgence comes easily. We often hear: "You owe yourself a little pleasure." From time to time, some Christians even attempt to offer biblical and theological arguments for their self-indulgence. These arguments usually spring from a distortion of the grace of God that makes grace a mere legal transaction rather than a life-transforming relationship to Christ.

In this selection, Puritan pastor John Flavel gives us a striking refutation of that dangerous assumption about salvation and appeals to a lifestyle that highlights Christlikeness, even in self-denial.

Flavel, like many Puritan leaders in seventeenth-century England, was tossed about by the violent events of the times. After his education at Oxford, he was ordained by a presbytery at Salisbury and entered the ministry at Devon. Later he moved to St. Saviour's Church at Dartmouth, but the restoration of the monarchy in 1660 and the new laws demanding conformity to the Church of England forced him into Nonconformity. In 1672, he gained a license to preach as a Congregationalist in his own house at Dartmouth. Just before his death, he led in a union of the Presbyterians and Congregationalists.

Devotees of the English Puritans have always admired Flavel's sermons because of their practical and warm-hearted tone. The following excerpt is from a volume that describes "how the Holy Spirit works."

ADVANTAGES IN BOTH WORLDS

"He that saith he abideth in him ought himself also so to walk, even as he walked" (1 John 2:6).

The life of Christ is the believer's copy, and though the believer cannot draw one letter exact as his copy is, yet his eye is still upon it; he is looking unto Jesus (Hebrews 12:2) and laboring to draw all the lines of his life as agreeably as he is able to Christ his pattern. . . .

The Christian's imitation of Christ, . . . necessarily implies that sanctification and obedience are the evidences of our justification and interest in Christ. Assurance is unattainable without obedience. "As many as walk according to this rule, peace be on them, and mercy, and upon the Israel of God" (Galatians 6:16). A careless conversation [or lifestyle] can never be productive of peace and consolation. . . . Let men talk what they may of the immediate sealing and comfort of the Spirit, without regard to holiness or obedience; sure I am, whatever delusion they meet with in that way, true peace and consolation are only to be expected and found in the imitation of Christ: "The fruit of righteousness shall be peace, and the effect of righteousness quietness and assurance for ever." We have it not for our holiness, but we always have it in the way of holiness. . . .

The self-denial of Christ is the pattern of believers, and their conformity to it is their indispensable duty. . . . "For ye know the grace of our Lord Jesus Christ, that though he was rich, yet for our sakes he became poor, that ye through his poverty might be rich" (2 Corinthians 8:9). Jesus Christ, for the glory of God and the love he bare to his people, denied himself all the delights and pleasures of the world. . . . Yet this was the least part of Christ's self-denial. What did he not give up when he left the bosom of his Father with the ineffable delights he there enjoyed from eternity, to drink the bitter cup of his Father's wrath for our sake! O Christians, look to your pattern and imitate your self-denying Savior.

Deny your natural self for him. Hate your own life, in competition with his glory, as well as your natural lusts. . . . Deny your civil self for Christ; whether it be gifts of the mind (Philippians 3:8) or your dearest relations in the world. . . . Deny your moral and religious self for Christ, your own righteousness (Philippians 3:9). Deny sinful self absolutely. . . .

To encourage you in this difficult work, consider what great things Christ denied for you, and what small matters you have to deny for him. How readily he denied all for your sakes, making no objections against the most difficult commands. How incapable you are of laying Christ under any obligation to deny himself in the least for you, and what strong obligations Christ has laid you under to deny yourselves in your dearest earthly interests for him. Remember that your self-denial is a condition consented to by yourselves if you ever received Christ aright. And consider how much your self-denial for Christ makes for your advantage in both worlds (Luke 18:29, 30). O therefore look not every man upon his own things, but upon the things that are of Christ.[26]

27

Working Humbly with God

BROTHER LAWRENCE (1610–1691)

F oxes have holes," Jesus once said, "and birds have nests, but the Son of Man has no place to lay his head" (Matthew 8:20). That was his way of pointing to his humble lifestyle. And the disciple is not above his master. In his insightful little volume *Christianity and History,* Herbert Butterfield, professor of Modern History at Cambridge, says, "Both in history and in life it is a phenomenon by no means rare to meet with comparatively unlettered people who seem to have struck profound spiritual depths." Perhaps the choice example of Butterfield's point is Nicholas Herman.

Nicholas Herman, better known as "Brother Lawrence," did nothing more sensational than talk with God in a monastery kitchen. Yet his reputation proved to be a source of encouragement to Christians for three hundred years.

Young Nicholas grew up in a meager home in Lorraine, France. Deprived of any formal education, he became a soldier and suffered a serious injury that left him lame. At the age of forty, he entered a Carmelite monastery in Paris as a layworker in the kitchen. There he remained with his pots and pans for the next forty years.

Conversations and letters from Brother Lawrence established his reputation as a spiritual guide. These were gathered and published after his death. We know them as *The Practice of the Presence of God.* Four conversations with Monsieur Beaufort, the Grand Vicar to Cardinal de Noailles, proved particularly helpful to Christians seeking a personal habit of communion with God. The following excerpt is from the fourth conversation.

GOD IN THE KITCHEN

Brother Lawrence often spoke to me with great fervour and frankness of his way of approaching God. He told me that it all amounted to one good act of renunciation of everything which we recognize does not lead to God, in order to habituate ourselves to an unbroken converse with him without mystery or artificiality. It is only necessary to realize that God is intimately present within us, to turn at every moment to him and ask for his help, recognize his will in all things doubtful, and to do well all that which we clearly see he requires of us, offering what we do to him before we do it, and giving thanks for having done it afterwards. In this unbroken communion one is continually preoccupied with praising, worshipping and loving God for his infinite acts of loving-kindness and perfection. . . .

When we are in doubt, God will never fail to give light when we have no other plan than to please him. Our sanctification does not depend upon some alteration in what we do, but in the doing for God what we commonly do for ourselves. It was lamentable, he said, to see how many people were set on doing certain things which they did only most imperfectly because of their many human preoccupations, always mistaking the means for the ends. He found the best means of drawing near God was through the common tasks which obedience laid down for him, purging them so far as lies in us from every human ingredient, and performing them all for the pure love of God.

It was, he said, enormous self-deception to believe that the time of prayer must be different from any other. We are equally bound to be one with God by what we do in our times of action as by the time of prayer at its special hour. His prayer was simply the presence of God, his soul unconscious of all else but love. But apart from such times he discovered scarcely any difference, keeping himself always near to God praising and blessing him with all his might, passing his life in unbroken joy, yet hoping that God would give him something to suffer when he should grow stronger. We should once for all, he said, trust ourselves to God, abandon ourselves to him alone, knowing that he would not deceive us. We must not grow weary in doing little things for the love of God, who looks not to the greatness of the deed, but to the love. Some failure at the start should not dismay us. Habit comes finally, and that produces the action without our thinking about it, and with wondrous joy.

He said that only faith, hope and love had to be nourished to become utterly dedicated to the will of God. All the rest was unimportant. . . . The goal which we must set before ourselves is to be in this life the most perfect worshippers of God possible, as we hope to be through all eternity.

When we undertake the spiritual life we should consider fundamentally what manner of people we are. Then we shall discover ourselves to be worthy of all contempt, unworthy of the name Christian, subject to all sorts of distress and numberless mischances which disturb us, and make us uneven in our health, moods, dispositions within and outside ourselves, in a word people whom God must bring low by boundless troubles and toils within and without. After that should we be amazed if troubles, temptations, opposition and contradiction of all kinds befall us in society? On the contrary we must submit to them and endure them as long as God shall please as experiences which are for our good. The higher the perfection to which a soul aspires the more dependent it is upon grace.[27]

28
Meditation

RICHARD BAXTER (1615–1691)

Stress was once a term reserved for structural engineers. In recent years, however, it has moved from engineering offices to fast-food restaurants. Everyone, it seems, has it and is trying to reduce it. One popular way to deal with stress is meditation. This often takes the form of some oriental religion, except that it magnifies technique and minimizes theology.

Christians, too, have more than a passing interest in meditation, but not as a tool for inward peace. The Christian lifestyle includes meditation as a soul-builder. It keeps our lives in tune with eternity.

Among Christian devotional coaches, none has written about meditation more helpfully than Richard Baxter. His time, like our own, were filled with uncertainty and stress. As we have noted, during the seventeenth century England fell into a civil war, saw its king beheaded, experienced a short-lived republic, and welcomed the return of the monarchy. Though deeply involved in all this, Baxter wrote *The Saints' Everlasting Rest*.

Despite his lack of university education, Baxter was ordained an Anglican priest in 1638 by the Bishop of Worcester, and from 1641 to 1660 he served a parish in Kidderminster. During the Civil War, pitting the monarchy against parliament, Baxter sided with the parliamentarians and acted as Oliver Cromwell's advisor for a time. He came to question some of Cromwell's aims, however, and welcomed the restoration of the monarchy in 1660.

When the government passed the new Act of Conformity in 1662, Baxter was forced out of the Church of England for his Nonconformist views and deprived of his living. When he continued to preach, he was imprisoned for fifteen months. He welcomed the Act of Toleration in 1689, which allowed him to preach again.

In addition to his devotional classic, *The Saints' Everlasting Rest*, Baxter also wrote *The Reformed Pastor*, a manual about pastoral leadership. Here are his recommendations for developing the habit of meditation.

ABOVE THE RATE OF OTHERS

The duty which I press upon thee so earnestly, . . . is, "The set and solemn acting of all the powers of thy soul in meditation upon thy everlasting rest."

This meditation is the acting of all the powers of the soul. It is the work of the living, not of the dead. . . . Men must necessarily have some relation to heaven before they can familiarly converse there. . . . And it must have all the powers of the soul to distinguish it from the common meditation of students; for the understanding is not the whole soul, and therefore cannot do the whole work. Christ and heaven have various excellencies, and therefore God hath formed the soul with different powers for apprehending these excellencies. . . . What good would language or music have done us, if we could not hear? or what pleasure should we have found in meats and drinks, without the sense of taste? So what good could all the glory of heaven have done us, or what pleasure should we have had in the perfection of God himself, if we had been without the affections of love and joy?

This meditation is upon thy everlasting rest. . . . It is joy, and not sorrow, that I persuade you to exercise. I urge you to look on no deformed objects, but only upon the ravishing glory of saints, and the unspeakable excellencies of the God of glory, and the beams that stream from the face of his Son. . . .

Frequency in heavenly contemplation is particularly important, to prevent a shyness between God and the soul. Frequent society breeds familiarity, and familiarity increases love and delight, and makes us bold in our addresses. . . . On the other hand, what a horror and discouragement will it be to the soul, when it is forced to fly to God in straits, to think, "Alas! I know not whither to go. I never went this way before. I have no acquaintance at the court of heaven. My soul knows not that God that I must speak to, and I fear he will not know my soul. . . ."

Be sure to enter upon this work with the greatest solemnity of heart and mind. There is no trifling in holy things. . . . Labor, therefore, to have the deepest apprehensions of the presence of God and his incomprehensible greatness. If Queen Esther must not draw near "till the king hold out the scepter," think, then, with what reverence thou shouldst approach Him who made the worlds with the word of his mouth, who upholds the earth as in the palm of his hand, who keeps the sun, moon and stars in their courses, and who sets the bounds to the raging sea! . . .

Consider, then, with what a spirit thou should meet the Lord, and with what seriousness and awe thou shouldest daily converse with him. Consider, also, the blessed issue of the work, if it succeed; it will be thy admission into the presence of God, and the beginning of thy eternal glory on earth; a means to make thee live above the rate of other men, . . . that thou mayest both live and die joyfully. . . . None on earth live such a life of joy and blessedness as those who are acquainted with this heavenly conversation. . . . How seriously, therefore, should this work be done![28]

Part 5

Saints in the Age of Revivals

A n incident aboard a ship at sea during January, 1736 provides us with a fitting illustration of the dominant note in the spiritual life during the eighteenth and nineteenth centuries. The good ship *Simmonds,* bound for Savannah, Georgia, headed into a series of violent Atlantic storms. The wind roared, the ship cracked and quivered, the waves lashed the deck.

A young, slightly built Anglican minister on board was terrified. John Wesley had preached the gospel to others but he was afraid to die. He was deeply awed, however, by a company of German believers called the Moravian Brethren. As the sea broke over the deck of the vessel, splitting the mainsail in pieces, the Moravians calmly sang their psalms to God.

Wesley wrote in his *Journal,* "This was the most glorious day I have ever seen."

That encounter aboard the *Simmonds* brings us to a new chapter in the story of the making of saints. We meet here the evangelical conviction that faith is not so much belief in all the right doctrine as it is an inward personal experience that enables the soul to trust in Christ, even in the face of death. The Moravians had it; Wesley did not. Not yet, but like many other Christians he soon found it in what we call the Evangelical Awakenings.

All the major leaders of the Protestant Reformation believed in the importance of a personal relationship with God. Martin Luther, for example, wrote, "If you have a true faith that Christ is your Savior, then at once you have a gracious God, for faith leads you in and opens up God's heart and will, that you should see pure grace and overflowing love."

In a similar way John Calvin defined faith as "a firm and solid confidence of the heart, by means of which we rest surely in the mercy of God which is promised to us through the Gospel."

THE TIMES

Unfortunately, powerful forces during the seventeenth century took their toll on the vibrant mood of the Reformation and replaced it with a cantankerous spirit of orthodoxy. By the middle of the seventeenth century,

Protestantism in Northern Europe was legal, acceptable, orthodox, and lifeless. Justification by faith was a doctrine to debate more than a life to experience.

A series of spiritual revivals, however, changed the face of Protestantism and gave fresh meaning to the term *evangelical*. In this period, the word "evangelical" came to mean more than acceptable doctrine. It also meant "born-again" Christianity, the experience of the Holy Spirit in a life-changing way.

The first signs of revival appeared in Germany in a movement called Pietism. Sparked by a pastor in Frankfurt, Philipp Jacob Spener and a university professor August Hermann Francke, Pietism stressed heartfelt faith through Bible study, prayer, and mutual care within the church. The name "pietist" came from their critics who hurled the term at them in derision of the piety engendered by their small-group meetings.

The Pietists, however, appealed to Luther and called for a return to his original emphasis on the gospel. They argued that men and women needed more than the doctrine of justification by faith. Like Luther they needed the justifying experience.

After Spener and Francke died, Pietist leadership fell to a German nobleman named Count Nicholas von Zinzendorf. On his estate in Saxony, he provided a haven for a refugee group called the Moravians. These were the believers Wesley met aboard the *Simmonds*.

When Wesley returned to England from Georgia as a first-term missionary drop-out, he was determined to find the Moravian secret of faith. In London he met Peter Bohler, a young Moravian pastor, who taught him that justification is a personal, life-transforming experience of God's forgiveness and a genuine believer can have it instantaneously.

That is what Wesley found on May 24, 1738. At a Moravian meeting on Aldersgate Street, he felt his heart strangely warmed. He felt for the first time in his life that he did trust in Christ alone for salvation.

Early the following year, in response to an invitation from his friend George Whitefield, Wesley entered the open fields near Bristol to preach to three thousand people and find his life's calling, the most prominent spokesman for England's greatest spiritual awakening.

Both of these movements, Pietism centered in Germany and the Wesley revival in Britain, drew upon earlier advocates of spiritual renewal. Spener freely confessed his admiration for the Lutheran pastor and devotional author, Johann Arndt and his *True Christianity*. And both Pietists and Wesleyans often expressed their admiration for Dutch and English Puritanism. The kinship of the movements is rather obvious in the simple definition of theology in the influential Puritan work *Marrow of Divinity* by William Ames. Theology, said Ames, is "the doctrine of Living to God."

Pietists and evangelicals insisted on the possibility of an authentic and personal experience of God. They stressed that the religious life was a life of love for God and man, marked by social sensitivity and ethical concern. To sustain their active life in the world, evangelicals stressed the importance of personal spirituality marked by early rising, prayer, and Bible study. William Wilberforce, the Member of Parliament who led in the overthrow of slave trade in the British Empire, spent two hours each day before breakfast in praying and studying his Bible. "Surely," he said, "the experience of all good men" is that "without a due measure of private devotions the soul will grow lean."

The following selections illustrate the multifaceted character of evangelicalism in Europe and America: personal holiness, missions, social concern, and supremely, Christ-honoring preaching. Something powerful had obviously been unleashed on the earth when men and women, even in an increasingly secular world, were willing to look beyond their own interests to offer the life of Christ to a dying world. Saints like the twelve here made the eighteenth and nineteenth centuries the age of the evangelical.

Remembering the Lord's Death

PHILIPP JACOB SPENER (1635–1705)

F rom time to time, someone points out that genuine Christianity is only one generation away from extinction. True faith simply cannot be passed on by institutions alone. Something must happen in people's hearts. That is why periodically some Christian or group of Christians asks, "What is the price for renewal in the church?"

Unfortunately, even renewal movements themselves tend to ossify, and in time, the renewal needs renewing. Many Protestants feel that is what happened to Protestantism. The creative generation of the Protestant Reformation was followed by a cautious period called Protestant scholasticism or confessionalism. Many of Luther's followers turned his robust faith into a dogma. Under the spell of the intellect, faith, as an act of surrender to the mercy of God revealed in Christ, was converted to mere assent to doctrinal truths set forth by scholars.

As we have noted, the seventeenth-century movement to reform the Reformation was called Pietism, and the earliest advocate of renewal in orthodox churches was Philipp Jacob Spener.

Spener grew up under strong religious influences, including the writings of Johann Arndt and the English Puritans. His ideas about heartfelt faith were strengthened at the University of Strassburg, where he met professors who understood Luther's justification by faith, not simply as a doctrine, but as a spiritual rebirth.

Spener's first ministry experience was in a pastorate at Strassburg, but after three years there, he accepted an invitation to Frankfurt. He was shocked by conditions in the town and he determined that the place to introduce change was in the church. He dared to call for repentance and discipleship. For several years, nothing significant happened. Then in 1669, he preached from the Sermon on the Mount, and people were converted and families reunited.

Encouraged, Spener gathered a little company of dedicated believers in his house twice a week for reading the Scriptures and religious discussion.

129

These meetings were soon scornfully dubbed "gatherings of the pious." That seems to be the birth of Pietism.

As interest in devotional literature grew, Spener sponsored the republication of Johann Arndt's *True Christianity*. He wrote an introduction for the book called *Pious Desires*, in which he spelled out several proposals for renewal in the churches. He recommended creation of Bible study groups for spiritual development, a strenuous Christian life, spiritual nurture for theological students, and simpler, Bible-based preaching.

Spener's idea was that renewal would spread if cell groups of experiential Christians could be gathered in congregations all over Germany. Enough dedicated Christians agreed with Spener to create the movement we call Pietism. It proved to be one of the most influential movements in modern Protestantism.

At the heart of Pietism's experiential faith was Christian meditation, and at the center of meditation was the reality of Christ's suffering. In one of his writings, Spener tells why this meditation is essential.

A DEEP AND PURE MIRROR

All the articles of our faith ought to be meditated upon with zeal, but there are some which are more important and more weighty than others and which are to be considered more often and with greater zeal.

Among these, however, there is none which is more necessary and more important than the article concerning the suffering and death of our Savior Jesus Christ. . . .

Since the suffering of Christ is a necessary suffering and occurred because of our sins, and for the reconciliation of our sins, we must meditate carefully upon it with heartfelt meditation upon our sins, which made such suffering necessary. Because Christ's suffering is a sufficient suffering through which divine justice was truly satisfied, we must look to it with faithful meditation on the deep use and fruit which we gain from it. Because the suffering of Christ is a holy suffering, directed in heartfelt obedience to the heavenly Father, we must look upon it with the same heartfelt intention to follow the example of that obedience in every way. Wherever such meditation is properly carried out, the results will follow. . . .

Both Augustine and Luther indicated that one is to look upon the sufferings of Christ in a twofold manner as a gift, the power and fruit of which are given to us for blessedness, and as an example. It is not enough that we grasp and look to it merely as a gift, but we must endeavor to look upon it as an example. As a result, it belongs to saving meditation on the sufferings that as often as one undertakes such meditation one is to think on those things which we see in Christ so that we may be like-minded with him and might truly and properly follow him. We are then clearly to see the whole life of Christ and particularly to see in his suffering a deep and pure mirror of the noblest and chief virtues.

We see in him first his obedience toward God his heavenly Father. . . . Moreover, we see in him his deep trust in his heavenly Father. . . . We also see the example of the thoughtful prayer of our loving Savior . . . and his patience, in suffering. . . .

Just as we see in the Lord Jesus great virtues which he manifested in his suffering toward his heavenly Father, likewise we see in that suffering those which he had toward men. . . . He manifested first by his whole suffering the warm love for us, since we can properly say that he was the Passover Lamb burned in the heat of love. The whole cause of that suffering was that Jesus loved us and could not help us in any way except through his sacrifice. As a result, he rather gave himself up to the deep and heaviest suffering rather than to allow us to lose our salvation. . . .

Our dear Savior purchased us with his sufferings as his own possession. This act binds us to him since we are no longer ourselves but are truly his; we may then no longer live according to our own will but must live completely for his pleasure. . . .

We must consider further that the suffering of Christ binds us to so much earnest practice of godliness, since through his suffering was won for us the power by which we are able to mortify our flesh and to conquer it; this power according to all our abilities we must make use of. . . .

This is the proper meditation on the suffering of Christ; it encourages all to further a repentant knowledge of sin and to follow faith and godliness.[29]

30

God's Use of Trials

FRANÇOIS FENELON (1651–1715)

T here is a spiritually deadening idea abroad today that says love always makes us happy. Applied to God it says, "God loves you and will always give you what you want." The dogma creates no end of doubt and depression when troubles overtake us. Since most of us have accepted "Smile, God loves you," we are thrown into confusion and anger when it seems that God is angry with us. What shall we do with trials? When we tumble from "cloud nine," do we have a resting place?

Most spiritual guides insist that we do, but we have to grow up if we want to find God's love in our troubles. François Fenelon is typical of these counselors.

Like most of us, Fenelon is an enigma. One author describes his puzzling personality in terms of a "baffling mixture of ecclesiastical authoritarianism and broad humanitarian ideals." He points to Fenelon's defense of papal infallibility on the one hand and his association with the mysticism of Madame Guyon on the other.

After his education under the Jesuits at Paris, Fenelon was ordained in 1675. He spent thirteen years attempting to reclaim Huguenots (French Protestants) for the Church of Rome. Then from 1689 to 1697, he served as tutor of Louis XIV's grandson, the Duke of Burgundy. At the height of his influence in 1695, he was named Archbishop of Cambrai.

Fenelon's troubles with the Church of Rome began when he met Madame Guyon and then defended her views on worship of God in silence and stillness of the soul. Pope Innocent XII condemned his book *Maxims of the Saints* and Fenelon was banished to his diocese at Cambrai. Only once in the next eighteen years did he leave Cambrai, but he sent letters of spiritual counsel to relatives, friends, priests, and all who turned to him for advice. Many of these contain almost a timeless quality because they speak to basic spiritual needs of people. Here is one of them that discusses spiritual trials.

THE DIMNESS OF FAITH

We have much trouble convincing ourselves of the kindness with which God crushes those he loves with crosses. Why take pleasure, we say, in making us suffer? Would he not know how to make us good without making us miserable? Yes, doubtless, God could do so, because nothing is impossible for him. He holds the hearts of men in his all-powerful hands, and turns them as he pleases, . . .

But God, who could have saved us without crosses, has not wished to do so. . . . In this he is the master. We have only to be silent, and to adore his profound wisdom without understanding it. What we see clearly is that we cannot become entirely good except as we become humble, disinterested, detached from ourselves, in order to relate everything to God without any turning back upon ourselves.

The operation of grace, which detaches us from ourselves and which uproots our self-love, cannot, without a miracle of grace, avoid being painful. God does not make miracles every day in the order of his grace, any more than in that of nature. . . . God hides his work, in the spiritual order under an unnoticeable sequence of events. It is thus that he keeps us in the dimness of faith. . . .

He uses the inconstancy, the ingratitude of his creatures, the disappointments and disgusts which we find in prosperity, to detach creatures from the deceitfulness of prosperity. He disillusions us with ourselves by the experiences of our weakness and our corruption, in an infinite number of failures. All this appears natural, and it is this sequence of apparently natural means that burns us in a slow fire. . . .

Why are we revolted by the long-drawn-out suffering? It is our attachment to ourselves, and it is this attachment which God wants to destroy. Because, while we still cling to ourselves, God's work is not accomplished. Then of what can we complain? Our trouble is being attached to the creature, and still more to ourselves.

God prepares a series of happenings which detaches us little by little from the creatures, and which at last tears us away from ourselves. The operation is painful, but it is our corruption which makes it necessary, and that is the cause of the pain we bear. If this flesh were healthy, the surgeon would not make any incision. He only cuts in proportion to the depth of the wound, and the area of the infection. Is it cruelty in the surgeon to cut to the quick? No, on the contrary, it is affection. It is skill. He would thus treat his only son.

God treats us in the same way. He never makes trouble for us except in spite of himself, so to speak. His father's heart does not try to desolate us. But he cuts to the quick to cure the ulcer of our heart. He has to take from us what we love too dearly, what we love in the wrong way and without discretion, what we love to the prejudice of his love.

What does he do about it? He makes us weep like children from whom we take the knife with which they are playing, and with which they could kill themselves. We weep, we are discouraged, we cry out loud. We are ready to murmur against God, as children vexed by their mothers. But God lets us cry, and saves us. He afflicts us only to correct us. . . .

O, how true it is then that God is good, that he is tender, that he is merciful to our true ills even when he seems to crush us, and even when we are tempted to pity ourselves because of his sternness.[30]

31

Yearning for God

ELIZABETH ROWE (1674–1737)

I have now done with mortal things," wrote Elizabeth Rowe as she faced death, "and all to come is vast eternity. Eternity! How transporting the sound! As long as God exists, my being and happiness is there secure. These unbounded desires, which the wide creation cannot limit, shall be satisfied for ever."

The thought was one she had often pursued. If eternity is not real, why do I have this insatiable thirst that nothing on earth can ever quench? It is a question devout Christians often ask.

Elizabeth Rowe was born Elizabeth Singer in Ilchester, England, the daughter of a Nonconformist minister. She began writing poetry at age twelve. Her imagination had, according to a friend, "a tincture of the muse almost from her childhood." Her soul seemed to be filled with sentiment and song. In her twenty-second year, she published, at the request of her friends, a collection of her poems.

She married Thomas Rowe in 1710, but after only five years of marriage, her husband died. The event moved her to write her most celebrated work, "Friendship in Death." Accepting her life of widowhood, she moved from London to Frome to devote herself to writing in a semi-reclusive life. Yet in every social situation, she seemed to radiate the love of God.

When she approached her own death, she wrote to her friend Isaac Watts, the well-known hymn writer, and asked him to edit her papers. He honored her request, and we have the reflection of Elizabeth Rowe's devotion to God in the little book titled *Devout Exercises of the Heart*. The *Devout Exercises*, said Watts, "are animated with such fire as seems to speak the language of holy passion." We offer here an excerpt, which reflects her yearning passion to love God more.

THIS HEAVENLY FLAME

Why, Oh my God, must this mortal structure put so great a separation between my soul and thee? I am surrounded with thy essence, yet I cannot perceive thee: *I follow thee, and trace thy footsteps in heaven and earth, yet I cannot overtake thee: thou art before me, and I perceive thee not.*

O thou, who, unseen, I love, by what powerful influence dost thou attract my soul? The eye has not seen thee, nor the ear heard, nor has it entered into the heart of man to conceive what thou art; and yet I love thee beyond all that the eye has seen, or my ear heard: beyond all that my heart can comprehend. . . .

My heart cleaves to thee, O Lord, as its only refuge, and finds in thee a secret and constant spring of consolation. I speak to thee with the utmost confidence, and think thy being my greatest happiness. The reflection on thy existence and greatness recreates my spirits, and fills my heart with alacrity: my soul overflows with pleasure: I rejoice, I triumph in thy independent blessedness and absolute dominion. Reign, O my God, for ever, glorious and uncontrolled!

I, a worm of the earth, would join my assent with the infinite orders above, with all the flaming ministers who rejoice in thy kingdom and glory. . . .

I love thee. Thus far I can speak, but all the rest is unutterable; and I must leave the pleasing tale untold, until I can talk in the language of immortality; and then I'll begin the transporting story, which shall never come to an end, but be still and still beginning; for thy beauties, O thou fairest of ten thousand! will still be new, and shall kindle fresh ardor in my soul to all eternity. . . .

Ye angels of God, who behold his face, explain to me the sacred mystery: tell me how this heavenly flame began, unriddle its wondrous generation. Who hath animated this mortal frame with celestial fire, and given a clod of earth this Divine ambition?

Ye flowery varieties of the earth, and ye sparkling glories of the skies, your blandishments are vain, while I pursue an excellence that casts a reproach on all your glory. I would fain close my eyes on all the various and lovely appearances you present, and would open them on a brighter scene. I have desires which nothing visible can gratify, to which no material things are suitable. O when shall I find objects more entirely agreeable to my intellectual faculties! My soul springs forward in pursuit of a distant good, whom I follow by some faint ray of light, which only glimmers by short intervals before me. O when will it disperse the clouds, and break out in full splendor on my soul!

But what will the open vision of the beauties effect, if, while thou art faintly imagined, I love thee with such a sacred fervor! to what blessed heights shall my admiration rise, when I shall behold thee in full protection—-when I shall see thee as thou art, exalted in majesty, and complete in beauty! how shall I triumph then in thy glory, and in the privileges of my own being! what ineffable thoughts will rise, to find myself united to the all-sufficient Divinity, by ties which the sons of men have no names to express! . . .

The league of nature shall be broken, and the laws of the mingled elements be cancelled; but my relation to the Almighty God shall stand fixed and unchangeable as his own existence: "Nor life, nor death, nor angels, nor principalities, nor powers, nor things present, nor things to come, shall ever separate me from his love.''

There are no limits to the prospects of my joy: . . . my bliss is without bounds: O when shall the full possession of it commence![31]

32

The Praises of God

PHILIP DODDRIDGE (1702–1751)

Praise is at the heart of the worship of God. Yet so often Christian prayers consist of "gimme" lists, rather than heartfelt praise. Can we change? How do we stimulate a deep sense of thanksgiving? How do we "magnify" God's name in our prayers? In his best-known book, Philip Doddridge gives us some specific suggestions about how to "tune the heart to sing God's praise."

Like other spiritual guides, Doddridge is probably better known to Christians today as a hymn writer. Some Christians still enjoy his

> O happy day that fixed my choice
> On Thee, my Savior and my God!
> Well may this glowing heart rejoice
> And tell its raptures all abroad.

During his lengthy ministry at Northampton, England (1729–1751), Doddridge stressed the training of students for an evangelical ministry. He stood between two ages. He was a Nonconformist leader in the modified Calvinistic tradition of Richard Baxter. But his call to heartfelt religion also linked him to the evangelicalism of the Methodist revival.

Some have suggested that Doddridge's *The Rise and Progress of Religion in the Soul* is the last great Puritan spiritual autobiography. That is less certain than its influence upon later generations of evangelicals. Few were changed more profoundly than William Wilberforce, the evangelical member of Parliament who led England's campaign against the slave trade. During a tour of the continent in 1784–1785, Wilberforce read Doddridge's book and experienced a spiritual crisis that made him a committed believer in "real Christianity."

Here is Doddridge's appeal to Christians to praise God.

BOW DOWN, HEIR OF GLORY

I would now suppose my reader to find, on an examination of his spiritual state, that he is growing in grace. And if you desire that this growth may at once be acknowledged and promoted, let me call your soul "to more affectionate exercise of love to God and joy in him," which suits, and strengthens, and exalts the character of the advanced Christian. . . . Spend not your sacred moments merely in confession or in petition, though each must have their daily share; but give a part, a considerable part, to the celestial and angelic work of praise. . . .

Come my Christian friend and brother, come and survey with me the goodness of our heavenly Father. . . .

Have you not reason to adopt the words of David, and say, "How many are thy gracious thoughts unto me, O Lord. How great is the sum of them. When I would count them, they are more in number than the sand."

Look back upon the path you have trod, . . . and say whether you do not . . . see all the road thick set with the marks and memorials of the divine goodness. Recollect the places where you have lived, and the persons with whom you have most intimately conversed, and call to mind the mercies you have received in those places, and from those persons, as the instruments of the divine care and goodness.

Recollect the difficulties and dangers with which you have been surrounded, and reflect attentively on what God has done to defend you from them, or to carry you through them. Think how often there has been but a step between you and death, and how suddenly God has sometimes interposed to set you in safety, even before you apprehended your danger. . . . Survey your circumstances in relative life; how many kind friends are surrounding you daily, and studying how they may contribute to your comfort. . . .

Reflect seriously on the state wherein divine grace found you: under how much guilt, under how much pollution; in what danger, in what ruin. Think what was, and O think, with yet deeper reflection, what would have been the case. The eye of God . . . saw you on the boarders of eternity, and pitied you; . . . and being merciful to you, he provided, in the counsel of his eternal love and grace, a Redeemer for you, and purchased you to himself, through the blood of his Son. . . . To accomplish these blessed purposes, he sent his grace into your heart. . . . He hath not only blessed you, but "made you a blessing.". . . Some in the way to heaven are praising God for you; and some perhaps, already there, are longing for your arrival, that they may thank you, . . .

Christian, look around on the numberless blessings of one kind and of another with which you are already encompassed, and advance your prospect still farther to what faith yet discovers within the veil. . . . Think of the rapture with which thou shalt attend his (Jesus') triumph in the resurrection-day, and receive this poor . . . body, transformed into his glorious image; and then think, "These hopes are not mine alone, but hopes of thousands and millions."

O Christian, thou art still intimately united and allied to them. Death cannot break a friendship thus cemented, and it ought not to render these insensible of the happiness of those friends for whose memory thou retainest so just an honor. They live to God as his servants; they "serve him, and see his face," and they make but a small part of that assembly. . . . And wilt thou not adore that God, who gives them all the superior glory of their more exalted nature, and gives them a heaven, which fills them with blessedness, . . .

This and infinitely more that this, the blessed God is, and was, and shall ever be. The felicities of the blessed spirits that surround his throne, and thy felicities, O Christian, are immortal. . . .

Bow down, O thou child of God, thou heir of glory—bow down, and let all that is within thee unite in one act of grateful love.[32]

A Glimpse of Glory

JONATHAN EDWARDS (1703–1758)

C hristian theologians, when speaking of God, often use such terms as "inexpressible," "ineffable," and "transcending." The saints show the same inability to put into words what their hearts have felt. They can only say that their worship of God was "like" the quenching of some thirst, or the embrace of some loved one, or the sight of some breathtaking splendor.

One interesting expression for a soul's encounter with God comes from the *Westminster Shorter Catechism,* written for the Westminster Assembly (1643–1647) convened during the English Civil War. It asks "What is the chief end of man?" And it answers "Man's chief end is to glorify God and to *enjoy* him forever." No one has struggled more valiantly to speak clearly of his "enjoyment" of God than the American colonial minister Jonathan Edwards.

Edwards was the precocious son of a Connecticut pastor. At eleven he had already written scientific papers about spiders and the rainbow. A year later he entered the new college at Yale and at twenty had secured his Master of Arts degree. The following year he served as a tutor at his alma mater. By this time he had also dedicated his life to God and served as a Presbyterian minister in New York.

In 1727, Edwards joined his grandfather, Solomon Stoddard, in the ministry of the Congregational Church at Northampton, Massachusetts. Here, in 1735–1737, largely as a result of his preaching, the town experienced a dramatic revival. In his book *A Faithful Narrative of the Surprising Work of God,* he described the transforming effect the revival had on the region. Three years later, New England felt the full impact of the Great Awakening through the preaching of George Whitefield.

Unfortunately, Edwards and his congregation disagreed over the standards for full membership in the church, and in 1750, he was forced to leave Northampton. He spent several years as a missionary to the Indians in a small frontier village called Stockbridge. These years, however, proved to be the most productive writing period of his life. His books about the freedom of the will, Christian ethics, and original sin, established his reputation as America's greatest theologian. In 1758, he was elected president of the College of New

Jersey at Princeton, but just before assuming his duties, he died of the newly developed inoculation for smallpox.

Edwards combined a brilliant mind with a quiet, contemplative personality. In 1739, he wrote an account of his own conversion and spiritual experience called *Personal Narrative*. The moving excerpt that follows reflects his struggle to express his "inexpressible" encounter with God.

THE SHEER ENJOYMENT OF GOD

The first instance, that I remember, of that sort of inward, sweet delight in God and divine things, that I have lived much in since, was on reading those words, 1 Tim. 1:17. Now unto the King eternal, immortal, invisible, the only wise God, be honour and glory for ever and ever, Amen. As I read the words, there came into my soul, and was as it were diffused through it a sense of the glory of the Divine Being; a new sense, quite different from any thing I ever experienced before.

Never had any words of Scripture seemed to me as these words did. I thought with myself, how excellent a Being that was, and how happy I should be, if I might enjoy that God, and be rapt up to him in heaven, and be as it were swallowed up in him for ever! I kept saying, and as it were singing, over these words of Scripture to myself; and went to pray to God that I might enjoy him, and prayed in a manner quite different than what I used to do; with a new sort of affection. But it never came into my thought, that there was any thing spiritual, or of a saving nature in this. . . .

The heaven I desired was a heaven of holiness; to be with God, and to spend my eternity in divine love, and holy communion with Christ. . . .

Holiness . . . appeared to me to be a sweet, pleasant, charming, serene, calm nature; which brought an inexpressible purity, brightness, peacefulness, and ravishment of the soul. . . . The soul of a true Christian . . . appeared like such a little white flower as we see in the spring of the year; low and humble on the ground, opening its bosom to receive the pleasant beams of the sun's glory; rejoicing as it were in a calm rapture; diffusing around a sweet fragrancy; standing peacefully and lovingly, in the midst of other flowers round about; all in the like manner opening their bosoms, to drink in the light of the sun. . . . My heart panted after this, to lie low before God, as in the dust; that I might be nothing, and that God might be ALL, that I might become as a little child. . . .

I have loved the doctrines of the gospel; they have been to my soul like green pastures. The gospel has seemed to me the richest treasure; the treasure that I have most desired, and longed that it might dwell richly in me. The way of salvation by Christ, has appeared, in a general way, glorious and excellent, most pleasant and most beautiful. It has often seemed to me, that it would, in great measure, spoil heaven, to receive it in any other way. . . .

Once, as I rode out into the woods for my health, in 1737, having alighted from my horse in a retired place, as my manner commonly has been, to walk for divine contemplation and prayer, I had a view, that for me was extraordinary, of the glory of the Son of God, as Mediator between God and man, and his wonderful, great, full, pure and sweet grace and love, and meek and gentle condescension. This grace appeared so calm and sweet, appeared also great above the heavens.

The person of Christ appeared ineffably excellent, with excellency great enough to swallow up all thought and conception—which continued, as near as I can judge, about an hour; which kept me the greater part of the time, in a flood of tears, and weeping aloud. I felt an ardency of soul to be, what I know not otherwise how to express, emptied and annihilated; to lie in the dust, and to be full of Christ alone; to love him with a holy and pure love; to trust him; to live upon him; to serve and follow him; and to be perfectly sanctified and made pure, with a divine and heavenly purity. I have, several other times, had views very much of the same nature, and which have had several effects.[33]

34

Mission to the Lost

DAVID BRAINERD (1718–1747)

Medical science has discovered certain people who are called "carriers." These are men and women capable of spreading an infectious disease without being, in a sense, infected themselves. They have no counterparts in Christianity. In the life of faith, "carriers" simply do not exist because people cannot catch the Christian faith from us unless we have it.

Evangelical saints, driven by this truth, have often demonstrated their devotion to Christ by missionary service. There are thousands of stories of personal sacrifice, but few accounts of missionary labors rival David Brainerd's *Journal* in its impact upon other lives.

Born near Hartford, Connecticut, in 1718, and orphaned at fourteen, Brainerd was apparently an outwardly pious young man. According to his own admission he "had a very good outside, and rested entirely on my duties." All that changed in 1739 when he had a profound conversion to Christ. He realized that his own piety was powerless to gain salvation, that only God's mercy could save him.

Shortly after his conversion, he entered Yale College, but was expelled in 1742 for an intemperate remark about a professor. He prepared for the ministry privately and was appointed a missionary to the American Indians by the Scottish Society for the Propagation of Christian Knowledge. He became a vital part of the colonial revival called "The Great Awakening."

Brainerd was a tireless witness to the Indians of eastern Pennsylvania and New Jersey. By November 1745, he had covered over three thousand miles on horseback through all sorts of weather. On occasion he would spend all day in prayer. Illness finally forced him to retire in the hopes of recovering. He died in Johnathan Edwards' home in New England.

Brainerd's *Journal,* which we are quoting here, inspired hundreds to volunteer for missionary service and had a profound effect on such leaders as Johnathan Edwards, John Wesley, William Carey and Henry Martyn. Even this brief excerpt reflects its power.

A GREAT AWAKENING

In the afternoon I preached to the Indians, their number was about sixty-five persons; men, women and children. I discoursed upon Luke 14:16–23, and was favored with uncommon freedom in my discourse. There was much visible concern among them, while I was discoursing publicly; but afterwards, when I spoke to one and another more particularly, whom I perceived under much concern, the power of God seemed to descend upon the assembly "like a mighty rushing wind," and with astonishing energy bore down all before it.

I stood amazed at the influence, which seized the audience almost universally; and could compare it to nothing more aptly than the irresistible force of a mighty torrent or a swelling deluge, that with its insupportable weight and pressure bears down and sweeps before it whatever comes in its way.

Almost all persons of all ages were bowed down with concern together, and scarcely one was able to withstand the shock of this surprising operation. Old men and women, who had been drunken wretches for many years, and some little children, not more than six or seven years of age, appeared in distress for their souls, as well as persons of middle age. . . . A principal man among the Indians, who before was the most secure and self-righteous, . . . and who with a great degree of confidence the day before told me "he had been a Christian more than ten years;" was now brought under solemn concern for his soul and wept bitterly. . . .

They were almost universally praying and crying for mercy in every part of the house, and many were out of doors; and numbers could neither go nor stand. . . .

Some of the white people who came out of curiosity to hear what "this babbler would say" to the poor ignorant Indians were much awakened; and some appeared to be wounded with a view of their perishing state. Those who had lately obtained relief were filled with comfort at this season. They appeared calm and composed, and seemed to rejoice in Christ Jesus. Some of them took their distressed friends by the hand, telling them of the goodness of Christ, and the comfort that is to be enjoyed in him; and thence invited them to come and give up their hearts to him. . . .

It is remarkable that God began this work among the Indians at a time when the least hope and, to my apprehension, the least rational prospect, of seeing a work of grace propagated amongst them. My hopes respecting the conversion of the Indians were perhaps never reduced to so low an ebb, since I had any special concern for them, as at this time. Yet this was the very season in which God saw fit to begin this glorious work! . . .

This great awakening, this surprising concern, was never excited by harangues of terror, but always appeared most remarkable when I insisted upon the compassion of a dying Savior, the plentiful provisions of the gospel, and the free offers of divine grace to needy, distressed sinners. . . .

Upon the whole, I think I may justly say that here are all the symptoms and evidences of a remarkable work of grace among the Indians, which can reasonably be desired or expected. May the great Author of this work maintain and promote the same here, and propagate it everywhere, till "the whole earth be filled with his glory!" Amen.[34]

35

Social Conscience

JOHN WOOLMAN (1720–1772)

I n the last three decades we have heard a lot about "social conscience." Not many Christians today challenge the idea that God intended Christianity for the marketplace and the public square. But are we entirely free from the assumption that a personal devotional life is a dead-end street? Piety and politics simply don't mix. All those images of President Lincoln and his Bible belong to a former age.

If that is so, where do we think Christians cultivate moral principles? Do they go to giant conventions? Or read another alarming book?

Dean Willard L. Sperry of Harvard once said, "If I were asked to date the birth of social conscience in its present form, I think I should put it on the twenty-sixth day of the eighth month of the year 1758—the day John Woolman in a public meeting verbally denounced Negro slavery." John Woolman believed that moral principles for society were formed in the conscience through the Bible and personal worship.

Woolman was born into a rather well-to-do Quaker family in colonial New Jersey. Though largely self-taught he entered the bakery business and did quite well at it until his increasing wealth began to trouble him. He turned to part-time tailoring and serving as a scribe or secretary for others. At the age of twenty-three he was also commissioned a Quaker "minister" and began traveling throughout the American colonies as a missionary. On these travels he spoke often of the sin of "holding fellow men in property." He felt this so deeply that a century before the Civil War in America, he predicted, "The seeds of great calamity and desolation are sown and growing fast on this continent."

We can trace the development of Woolman's social conscience in his *Journal,* which has become a classic in American literature.

ACTING ON INWARD PRINCIPLES

About the twenty-third year of my age, I had many fresh and heavenly openings, in respect to the care and providence of the Almighty over his creatures in general, and over man as the most noble amongst those which are visible. And being clearly convinced in my judgment that to place my whole trust in God was best for me, I felt renewed engagements that in all things I might act on inward principle of virtue, and pursue worldly business no further than as truth opened my way.

About the time called Christmas I observed many people, both in town and from the country, resorting to public-houses, and spending their time in drinking and vain sports, tending to corrupt one another; on which account I was much troubled. In one house in particular there was much disorder; and I believed it was a duty incumbent on me to speak to the master of that house. I considered I was young, and that several elderly friends in town had opportunity to see these things; but though I would gladly have been excused, yet I could not feel my mind clear.

The exercise was heavy; and as I was reading what the Almighty said to Ezekiel, respecting his duty as a watchman, the matter was set home more clearly. With prayers and tears I besought the Lord for his assistance, and He, in loving-kindness, gave me a resigned heart. At a suitable opportunity I went to the public-house; and seeing the man amongst much company, I called him aside, and in the fear and dread of the Almighty expressed to him what rested on my mind. He took it kindly, and afterwards showed more regard to me than before. In a few years afterwards, he died, middle-aged; and I have often thought that had I neglected my duty in that case it would have given me great trouble; and I was humbly thankful to my gracious Father, who supported me herein.

My employer, having a Negro woman, sold her, and desired me to write a bill of sale, the man being waiting who bought her. The thing was sudden; and though I felt uneasy at the thoughts of writing an instrument of slavery for one of my fellow-creatures, yet I remembered that I was hired by the year, that it was my master who directed me to do it, and that it was an elderly man, a member of our Society [of Friends], who bought her; so through weakness I gave way, and wrote it; but at the executing of it I was so afflicted in my mind, that I said before my master and the Friend that I believed slave-keeping to be a practice inconsistent with the Christian religion. This, in some degree, abated my uneasiness; yet as often as I reflected seriously upon it I thought I should have been clearer if I had desired to be excused from it, as a thing against my conscience; for such it was.[35]

36
The New Birth

JOHN WESLEY (1703–1791)

The evangelical tradition in Christianity has always insisted that the first words that men and women must utter to God are, "I'm sorry." In other words, they must repent . . . and believe the gospel, the Good News. That experience, marked by repentance of sin and faith in Jesus Christ, is called "the new birth." It is the prerequisite of all acceptable devotion.

But what is "the new birth"? Thousands have offered answers to that question, but none so well as John Wesley, who knew both the doctrine and the experience.

"A brand plucked from the burning." That is the way Wesley described God's hand upon his life as he recalled a childhood event at the age of six. The Anglican rectory at Epworth, England, where his father was minister, burned to the ground. Left alone amid the flames on the second floor, John was saved when a neighbor saw him in a window.

For 30 years Wesley was uncertain of God's purpose for his life. His saintly mother, Susanna, and books like *The Imitation of Christ* and Jeremy Taylor's *Holy Living and Dying* made a deep impression upon him, but as a student at Oxford his religion was all form and little power. He participated in a "Holy Club" to improve his religion and even volunteered for missionary service in the Georgia colony, but he had no assurance of God's forgiveness until one night shortly after he returned from America.

On May 24, 1738, while listening to the reading of Luther's preface to the epistle to the Romans, he felt his heart "strangely warmed." And he received an assurance that Christ had taken away his sins. Shortly after this encounter, at the invitation of his friend George Whitefield, Wesley entered the open fields, preaching to the working classes of England. No one was more surprised at the results than Wesley. Thousands responded to his invitation to Christ, and Wesley found his life's calling.

To encourage new converts Wesley formed small "classes" (in the Latin sense of "divisions" of the young movement) for spiritual development. Many lay preachers emerged from these groups and soon conferences of these preachers were necessary. The whole movement, energized by Wesley's preaching and direction, came to be called the Methodist revival.

As long as Wesley lived, he resisted any separation from the Anglican Church. But shortly after he died, the Methodist Church joined the growing list of modern denominations and added its own distinctive witness to evangelical Christianity.

Here is Wesley's description of the central experience of the Methodist revival.

ALIVE UNTO GOD

Before a child is born into the world he has eyes, but sees not; he has ears, but does not hear. He has a very imperfect use of any other sense. He has no knowledge of any of the things of the world, or any natural understanding. To that manner of existence which he then has, we do not even give the name of life. It is then only when a man is born, that we say he begins to live. For as soon as he is born, he begins to see the light, and the various objects with which he is encompassed. His ears are then opened, and he hears the sounds which successively strike upon them. At the same time, all the other organs of sense begin to be exercised upon their proper objects. He likewise breathes, and lives in a manner wholly different from what he did before.

How exactly doth the parallel hold in all these instances? While a man is in a mere natural state, before he is born of God, he has in a spiritual sense, eyes and sees not; a thick impenetrable veil lies upon them; he has ears, but hears not; he is utterly deaf to what he is most of all concerned to hear. His other spiritual senses are all locked up; he is in the same condition as if he had them not. Hence he has no knowledge of God; in intercourse with him; he is not at all acquainted with him. He has no true knowledge of the things of God, either spiritual or eternal things; therefore, though he is a living man, he is a dead Christian.

But as soon as he is born of God, there is a total change in all these particulars. The "eyes of his understanding are opened" . . . and he who of old "commanded light to shine out of darkness" shining on his heart, he sees the light of the glory of God, his glorious love, "in the face of Jesus Christ." His ears being opened, he is now capable of hearing the inward voice of God, saying "Be of good cheer, thy sins are forgiven thee" and "Go and sin no more.". . . He feels "the love of God shed abroad in his heart by the Holy Ghost which is given unto him"; and all his spiritual senses are then exercised to discern spiritual good and evil. . . . And now he may be properly said to live: God having quickened him by his Spirit, he is alive unto God through Jesus Christ.

A WORLD VISION

Suffer me now to tell you my principles in this matter. I look upon all the world as my parish; thus far I mean, that in whatever part of it I am, I judge it meet, right and my bounden duty to declare, unto all that are willing to hear, the glad tidings of salvation. This is the work which I know God has called me to, and sure I am that His blessing attends it. Great encouragement have I, therefore, to be faithful in fulfilling the work he hath given me to do. His servant I am; and, as such, am employed . . . according to the plain direction of his word—"as I have opportunity, doing good unto all men." And his providence clearly concurs with His word, which has disengaged me from all things else that, I might singly attend in this very thing, "and go about doing good."[36]

37

Fashionable Christianity

HANNAH MORE (1745–1833)

O ne moment of reflection while watching television should convince most of us that the American economy runs in large part on a passion to be "in style." The whole idea seems to be a conspiracy of a handful of marketing experts in New York City, but it feeds on the fears of people whose greatest dread in life is to be wearing the wrong jacket or ordering the wrong drink. The word for that fear is "worldliness."

The saint who understood worldliness most profoundly and analyzed it most helpfully was the English writer, Hannah More. She was born near Bristol and exhibited early an unusual range of literary and artistic skills. An unexpected settlement gave her the financial independence she needed to move to London and enter the literary scene. As an admired author and playwright she met the rich and famous, including Samuel Johnson, Horace Walpole, and David Garrick.

Something happened in 1779, however, to turn her life in another direction. She left the stage and devoted her energies and talents to evangelistic and philanthropic labors. Her new associates, especially John Newton, Henry Thornton, and William Wilberforce, were leaders of evangelical causes in England. She wrote pamphlets in support of the anti-slavery campaign led by Wilberforce in Parliament. And she joined her sisters in pioneering in the organizaiton of schools for poor children and self-improvement clubs for their mothers.

Her writings in her later years are markedly more devotional than her early ones. Among these is one titled *The Spirit of Prayer,* and one addressing *Strictures on the Modern System of Female Education.* In this last one she probes the character of worldliness and its passion for "style."

THE WORLDLY SPIRIT

It is humorous to hear complaints against the strictness of a life of faith coming from persons who voluntarily pursue a life made infinitely more laborious by attempts to be always fashionable. How really burdensome

159

would Christianity be if it required such attention to style, such unremitting labors, such a succession of efforts!

A worldly spirit—by which I mean simply a disposition to prefer worldly pleasures, worldly satisfactions and worldly advantages to the immortal interest of the soul—is not (like almost any other fault) the effect of passion or the consequence of surprise when the heart is off guard. . . . Rather, it is the spirit, soul and living principle of evil. . . .

We have great ardor in carrying on our worldly projects, because we believe the good which we are pursuing is real and will reward the trouble of the pursuit . . . But where we see persons professing a lively faith in a better world, yet laboring little to obtain an interest in it, can we avoid suspecting that their belief (not only in their title to eternal happiness, but in eternal happiness itself) is not very well grounded. . . ?

Even that very taste for enjoyment which leads the persons in question to . . . acquire talents which may enable them to relish the pleasures of a stylish life should induce those who are really looking for a future state of happiness to acquire something of the taste, disposition and talents which prepare them for its enjoyment. Neglecting to do this must proceed from one of these two causes: either they must think their present course a safe and proper one, or they must think that death will produce some sudden and surprising alteration in their human character.

But the office of death is to transport us to a new state, not to transform us to a new nature. The stroke of death is intended to effect our deliverance out of this world and our introduction into another, but it is not likely to effect any sudden and surprising total change in our hearts or our tastes. In fact, we are assured in Scripture that "he that is filthy will be filthy still, and he that is holy will be holy still."

It is awful to reflect that such a spirit as we have allowed predominance here will be maintained forever, that just as the will is when we close our eyes upon the things of time, so also will it be when we open them on those of eternity. . . . If we die with our hearts running over with love for the world, there is no promise to lead us to expect that we shall rise with hearts full of the love of God. Death indeed will expose us to ourselves such as we are, but it will not make us such as we are not. . . .

When the curtain is drawn up at the theatre, though it serves to introduce us to the entertainment behind it, it does not create in us any new faculties to understand or enjoy the entertainment. These must have been already long in the acquiring; they must have been provided beforehand and brought with us to the theatre if we are to appreciate the pleasures of the place, for entertainment can only operate on the taste we bring to it. It is too late to be acquiring when we ought to be enjoying. . . .

While we would with deep humility confess that we cannot purchase heaven by any works or qualifications of our own, and gratefully acknowledge that it must be purchased for us by "Him who loved us and washed us from our sins in his blood," yet let us remember that we have no reason to expect we could be capable of enjoying the pleasure of a heaven thus purchased without first being heavenly-minded. . . .[37]

38

Suffering

ROBERT MURRAY McCHEYNE (1813–1843)

J ob, the ancient patriarch who knew what he was talking about, once said, "Man born of woman is of a few days and full of trouble."
Not many of us are prepared to argue with him, because not many of us escape troubles. They come in all shapes and sizes. The important question is, when they come, what do we do about them?

Troubles always pose special problems for those Christians who believe that life holds no genuine accidents, that God is in control of everything that comes our way. I say that is a special problem because these Christians tend to ask, "What is God doing in this painful situation?" Many times they find no clear answer to the question. That is when pastors, like Robert Murray McCheyne, have to minister to people with these painful question marks.

Like his fellow countryman, Henry Scougal, Robert Murray McCheyne lived only twenty-nine years, but in that time he made a profound impact. He attended the University of Edinburgh during the days of popular Thomas Chalmers, but the death of his older brother seems to have made the greatest change in his life. "I lost my loved and loving brother," he wrote "and began to seek a Brother who cannot die."

In 1835, young McCheyne was licensed to preach by the Presbytery of Annon, and the next year he was ordained and received an invitation to the ministry at St. Peter's Church at Dundee, a congregation of about eleven hundred. His preaching reflected his inner life. He began each day at an early hour with personal worship and the reading of devotional literature, such as *The Letters of Samuel Rutherford,* Baxter's *Call to the Unconverted,* and Jonathan Edward's *The Life of David Brainerd.*

Through his seven brief years of public ministry McCheyne was troubled by poor health. Early in 1843, he conducted a mission in England and Aberdeenshire. Upon his return he came down with a serious illness. Apparently while visiting some people sick with the fever, he had caught the infection himself. On March 25 he died and was buried by St. Peter's Church.

In 1844, McCheyne's friend Andrew A. Bonar collected and published the popular young minister's letters, sermons, and other papers. During the next century the circulation of the memoirs was little short of phenomenal. In view of his suffering and short life, we have selected here one of his letters to his church people in which he looks for God's work through "providences."

COMFORT FOR THE AFFLICTED

Edinburgh, February 13, 1839

To all of you, my dear friends and people, who are and shall ever be followers of the Lamb, whithersoever He goeth, your pastor again wishes you grace and peace from God our Father, and the Lord Jesus Christ. . .

In Job 23:8–10 you will find these solemn words: "Behold, I go forward, but he is not there; and backward, but I cannot perceive him . . . But he knoweth the way that I take: when he hath tried me, I shall come forth as gold."

You have here . . . a child of light walking in darkness—an afflicted soul seeking, and seeking in vain, to know why God is contending with him.

Dear friends, this is not an uncommon case; even to some of you God's providences often appear inexplicable. . . . Perhaps more than one trouble has come upon you at a time—wave upon wave, thorn upon thorn. Before one wound was healed, another came, before the rain was well away, "clouds returned." You cannot explain God's dealings with you, you cannot get God to explain them; . . .

God does many things to teach us that He is God, and to make us wait upon Him. . . . "He knoweth the way that I take." What sweet comfort there is in these words: He that redeemed me—He that pities me as a father—He who is the only wise God—He whose name is love—"He knoweth the way that I take."

God has called you to suffer, and you go, like Abraham, not knowing whither you go. . . .Still, be of good cheer, suffer with Christ! God marks your every step. . . .He that loves you with an infinite, unchanging love, is leading you by His Spirit and providence. He knows every stone, every thorn in your path. . . .

"When he hath tried me, I shall come forth as gold." This also is precious comfort. There will be an end of your affliction. . . .

But shall we come out the same way we went in? Ah, no! "We shall come out like gold.". . . .Affliction will certainly purify a believer. . . . Ah, how much dross there is in every one of you, dear believers, and in your pastor! . . .Oh that all the dross may be left behind in the furnace! What imperfection, what sin, mingles with all we have ever done! . . .We shall come out like gold. We shall shine more purely as "a diadem in the hand of our God." We shall become purer vessels to hold the sweet-smelling incense of praise and prayer. We shall become holy golden vessels for the Master's use in time and in eternity. . . .

My chief comfort concerning you is that "my God shall supply all your need according to his riches in glory by Christ Jesus." Brethren, farewell! Be perfect, be of good comfort, be of one mind, live in peace, and the God of love and of peace shall be with you.[38]

39

Personal Holiness

PHOEBE PALMER (1807–1874)

I n his arresting little book *He Is Able,* Will Sangster says it is pride that makes a person rebel against his place in the universe. It dethrones the Creator in the heart of man and puts self in the center. "It struts, and shouts, and brags." It makes "the puffed-up little ego the pole of all things." "If men only knew the thousand sins which pride begets, they would hate it for the devilish thing it is." It is hell to have self in the center of life.

If Sangster is right—and who is prepared to argue the point?—then personal holiness must begin with the overthrow of pride and self-will. That was the central message of the evangelical holiness preachers in the last half of the nineteenth century.

The quest for perfect sanctification or holiness is as old as Christianity, but in nineteenth-century England and America millions of Christians joined in the pursuit with unusual passion. Holiness doctrine was of two types: Wesleyan and Keswick. The first reflected John Wesley's teaching on "perfectionism" but looked for an instantaneous change wrought by a "second blessing" from the Holy Spirit—second, of course, to the initial "new birth" from the Spirit.

The other type of holiness was called the Keswick doctrine after the conferences in England where the views were initially promoted. Keswick speakers tried to avoid the entire sanctification or "second blessing" emphasis of the Wesleyan speakers in favor of a "crisis" of surrender and a day by day process of trust in the power of God for victory over sin.

Among the Wesleyan holiness speakers was an unusually effective lady, Mrs. Phoebe Palmer. Born in New York City, Phoebe was married at nineteen to Walter Palmer, a physician who shared her spiritual hunger. After the death of two sons within weeks of their births, the Palmers dedicated their energies to religious activities.

On July 26, 1837, Phoebe had an experience of total surrender to God, which she identified as "entire sanctification." The depth of her conviction and the vividness of her experience made Phoebe Palmer an extremely effective advocate of personal holiness. For 40 years she lead "The Tuesday

Meeting for the Promotion of Holiness" in her parlor. Many men as well as women professed entire sanctification there. She also proved to be an unusually powerful speaker at camp meetings and revival services.

The paragraphs that follow give her own account of her entrance into "entire sanctification."

UNCONDITIONAL SURRENDER

The state of my mind for years, as nearly as I can express it, was this—I had rather a belief that I was a child of God; yet I had not enough of the spirit of adoption to cry with unwavering confidence, "Abba, Father." O how often did I feel a longing thirst for holiness, conscious that nothing less could supply my need! . . .

Thus I continued to rise and fall, and consequently made but little progress on my way to heaven, until the early part of last June when, in the strength of Omnipotence, I resolutely determined that I would set myself apart wholly for God, fully purposed that my ceaseless aim should thenceforth be the entire devotion of my powers to the service of the Redeemer. . . . I calmly counted the cost, which I felt would be the surrender of my own will in all things. . . .

From the time I made the resolve to be wholly devoted to the service of Christ, I began to feel momentarily that I was being built up and established in grace: humility, faith, and love, and all the fruits of the Spirit, seemed hourly maturing. . . .

One exercise which I then commenced, I will mention:—It was that of making daily, in form and in the most solemn manner, a dedication of all the powers of body and soul, time, talents, and influence to God.

Thus I continued to enjoy increasing happiness in God, but not yet perfectly satisfied as to the witness—the indubitable seal of consecration. I was kept in constant expectation of the blessing.

July 26. On the morning of this day, . . . my thoughts rested more especially upon the beloved one whom God had given to be the partner of my life. How truly a gift from God, and how essentially connected with my spiritual, as also my temporal happiness, is this one dear object! I exclaimed.

Scarcely had these suggestions passed, when with keenness these inquiries were suggested: "Have you not professedly given up all for Christ? If he who now so truly absorbs your affections were required, would you not shrink from the demand?" I need not say that this dear object, though often in name surrendered, was not in reality given up. . . .

My impression was, that the Lord was about to take my precious husband from me. The inquiry with me was, whether it were possible that my heavenly Father could require me to make the surrender, when he had authorized my love, by making it my duty to be of one heart and soul with him. But grace interposed; and from more mature consideration, I was led to regard it as extraordinary condescension in God thus to apprise me of his designs, by way of preparing my heart for the surrender. . . .

Truth in the inward part I now in verity apprehended as God's requirement. Grace triumphed. In full view of the nature of the sacrifice, I said, "Take life or friends away."

. . . I could now as easily have doubted of my existence as to have doubted God was the supreme object of my affections. . . . Let my spirit from thenceforth ceaselessly return to the God that gave it. Let this body be actuated by the Spirit, as an instrument in thy hand for the performance of thy pleasure in all things. I am thine—wholly thine. Thou dost now reign in my heart unrivaled. Glory! Glory be to the Father, Son, and Holy Ghost, forever! . . .

While thus exulting, the voice of the Spirit again appealingly applied to my understanding, "Is not this sanctification?" I could no longer hesitate; reason as well as grace forbade; and I rejoiced in the assurance that I was wholly sanctified—throughout body, soul, and spirit.[39]

40

Losses

CHARLES HADDON SPURGEON (1834–1892)

T ough times come to everyone. In our day we have an ample supply of tranquilizers—insurance policies, drugs, psychologists, religions, alcohol, sex. But nothing can erase the fact that adversities come with living.

One of the most popular preachers of the nineteenth century often reminded his listeners to expect troubles, even in the Gilded Age. I mean, of course, Charles Haddon Spurgeon.

It was especially important to make the point in Spurgeon's day because the nineteenth century was supposed to be the "Age of Progress." Optimism was in the air. Spurgeon, however, knew the Bible too well and preached it too faithfully to ignore the storms of life.

Spurgeon was the son and grandson of Independent (or Congregationalist) pastors. He was converted, however, in a Primitive Methodist chapel. Snowy weather, early in 1850, compelled him to take refuge in the modest building and face the direct appeal of the lay preacher to "look to Christ." The experience changed young Spurgeon's life.

After baptism he began preaching, though only a teenager, and became pastor of Waterbeach Baptist Chapel. Three years later, in 1854, he accepted a call to Park Street Baptist Chapel in south London. Spurgeon's clear voice, mastery of the English language, sense of humor, and grasp of the Scriptures made him a popular and effective preacher. The Park Street Chapel was soon overflowing, so the congregation, in 1859, erected the spacious Metropolitan Tabernacle. During Spurgeon's 38 years of ministry in London the church received nearly 15,000 members.

The pulpit, however, was only the heart of Spurgeon's ministry. He reached out to the city by founding an orphanage, a college for pastors, a colportage association, and temperance, mission, and clothing societies.

Thanks to the printed page, Spurgeon's books and sermons were distributed throughout the world. To this day hundreds of pastors draw inspiration and ideas from his writings. Here are two short examples of his power with words.

WHEN WINTER COMES

While the earth remaineth, seedtime and harvest, and cold and heat, and summer and winter, and day and night shall not cease (Genesis 8:22).

I have seen in our mortal life summer and winter, prosperity and adversity. Do not expect, dear brother, while you are in this world, always to dwell among the lilies and roses of prosperity. Summer will come, and you will be wise to make hay while the sun shines by using all opportunities for usefulness; but look for winter.

I do not know into what trade you can enter to be secure against losses, nor what profession you could follow in which you would escape disappointments. I know no corner of the earth without its night, no land without its stones, no sea without its storms. As to spiritual and mental experience, it seems to me within myself that while earth remains I will have ebbs and flows, my rising and my sinkings. Do not therefore begin to kick and quarrel with the dispensations of God's providence. When it is summertime say, "The Lord gave, and blessed be His name." When it is winter say, "The Lord hath taken away, and blessed be His name." Keep to the same music, even though you sometimes have to pitch an octave lower. Still praise and magnify the Lord whether you be sowing or reaping. Let Him do what seems good to Him, but to you let it always seem good to praise.

Many are the afflictions of the righteous: but the Lord delivereth him out of them all (Psalm 34:19).

Losses, too, are frequently the means God uses to fetch home His wandering sheep; like fierce dogs, they bring wanderers back to the shepherd. How often have we seen the Christian rendered obedient to his Lord's will by straightness of bread and hard labor. When rich and increased in goods, many professors carry their heads much too loftily, and speak much too boastfully. Like David, they boast: "My mountain standeth fast; it shall never be moved." When the Christian grows wealthy, is in good repute, has good health, and a happy family, he too often wanders away. If he be a true child of God, there is a rod preparing for him.

We never live so well as when we live on the Lord Jesus simply as He is, and not upon our enjoyments and raptures. Faith is never more likely to increase in strength than in times which seem adverse to her. When she is lightened of trust in joys, experiences, frames, feelings, and the like, she rises the nearer heaven. Trust in your Redeemer's strength, benighted soul; exercise what faith you have, and by and by He shall rise upon you with healing beneath His wings. Go from faith to faith and you shall receive blessing upon blessing.[40]

41
Thirst for God

GEORGE MATHESON (1842–1906)

In its highest form, love blends into grace. It accepts not the achievement of the loved one but the desire. It makes something good and beautiful out of life's failures. Love in this sense transforms even suffering into an asset. How do we know that? We see it so clearly in God's love for us.

The hymn writer has captured the thought in these moving lines:

O Love that wilt not let me go,
I rest my weary soul in Thee;
I give Thee back the life I owe,
That in Thine ocean depths its flow
May richer, fuller be.

O Joy that seekest me through pain,
I cannot close my heart to Thee;
I trace the rainbow through the rain,
And feel the promise is not vain
That morn shall tearless be.

O Cross that liftest up my head,
I dare not ask to fly from Thee;
I lay in dust life's glory dead,
And from the ground there blossoms red,
Life that shall endless be.

Many Christians who know nothing about George Matheson have met him through this well-known hymn, "O Love That Wilt Not Let Me Go." The lines reflect Matheson's own spiritual quest. The words came to him in five short minutes during his fortieth year, but they came to a man practically blind since his eighteenth year.

In spite of his handicap, Matheson graduated with honors from Glasgow University in his native Scotland. He was ordained to preach at the age of twenty-four and served in Glasgow and Innellan before moving to St. Bernard's Church in Edinburgh.

Matheson was an influential preacher and author. He published theologi-

173

cal volumes as well as a collection of hymns and devotional works. We can trace his insights into the love of God in two excerpts from his little book *My Aspirations*.

A CRY FOR RIGHTEOUSNESS

"Blessed are they which do hunger and thirst after righteousness: for they shall be filled"(Matthew 5:6).

What a wonderful breadth of divine charity! He who is altogether righteous will accept from us even the thirst for righteousness. He will not reserve his blessing until I become actually pure; he will bless my very effort after purity. He will accept the mere desire of him; the mere wish of my heart to be like him; the mere throb of my pulse to be near him. Though I have not reached him, if only I see in him a beauty that I long for, he will count it unto me for righteousness. Though I claim not to be like him, and despair even to touch the hem of his garment, if only I can admire afar off the kingliness of his beauty, he will bless my very hunger and my very thirst for him.

Yet say not, Oh my soul, that thou hast salvation without goodness. Thou couldst not hunger after him, thou couldst not thirst for him, if he were not already in thee. . . . If thou were not like him, thou wouldst not see him as he is. If he were not in thee thou couldst not wish to imitate him—couldst not even feel the despair of imitating him.

Thou canst not admire what is out of thy nature, nor seek what is not kindred to thy being. . . . Thou canst cry out for outward food before thou knowest the taste thereof, but thou canst not cry for righteousness until thou has "tasted that the Lord is good." He who sees the King in his beauty has himself begun to be beautiful; he who hungers and thirsts after righteousness is already beginning to be filled.

THE GIFT OF SUFFERING

"Thou hast enlarged me when I was in distress" (Psalm 4:1).

This is one of the grandest testimonies ever given by man to the moral government of God. It is not a man's thanksgiving that he has been set free from suffering. It is a thanksgiving that he has been set free through suffering: "Thou hast enlarged me when I was in distress." He declares the sorrows of life to have been themselves the source of life's enlargement. And have not you and I a thousand times felt this to be true? It is written of Joseph in the dungeon that "the iron entered into his soul." We all feel that what Joseph needed for his soul was just the iron. He had seen only the glitter of the gold. . . . We need the iron to enlarge our nature. The gold is but a vision; the iron is an experience. The chain which unites me to humanity must be an iron chain. That touch of nature which makes the world akin is not joy, but sorrow; gold is partial, but iron is universal.

My soul, if thou wouldst be enlarged into human sympathy, thou must be narrowed into the limits of human suffering; Joseph's dungeon is the road to Joseph's throne. . . . It is thy limit that is thine enlargement. It is the shadows of thy life that are the real fulfillment of thy dreams of glory. Murmur not at the shadows; they are better revelations than thy dreams. . . . The door of thy prison-house is a door into the heart of the universe. God has enlarged thee by the binding of sorrow's chain.[41]

42

The Higher Christian Life

HANNA WHITALL SMITH (1832–1911)

I sn't it true that some Christians seem to live on a higher spiritual level than others? Aren't there people who go to church on Sunday, and may even contribute regularly to its support, but who reveal nothing else to distinguish them from people who have no interest in religion at all? They worry, get irritable, show pride, and lose their tempers just like people who laugh at religion. But aren't there other Christians who light up a room, who seem to have some secret of poise or inner happiness? They never speak critically of anyone else, and seldom talk about themselves, and they listen when you are talking to them as though your thoughts were the most interesting they had heard all day long.

These are the questions that lead Christians into "holiness" movements. As we have seen, the nineteenth century generated widespread interest in holiness. Most of the movements looked back to John Wesley for their inspiration. But some arose from men and women who could claim their own special touch from God. One of these was Hanna Whitall Smith.

The daughter of a pious Philadelphia Quaker family, Hannah Whitall suffered from depression and doubt during her adolescent years. In 1858, however, when she came to faith through the Plymouth Brethren movement, she was delivered from her doubts. During that same year Robert Pearsall Smith was converted through a Presbyterian ministry. The two of them soon met and were married.

In 1867, Hannah came to a fresh understanding of spiritual victory while reading the words in Romans 6:6, "that we should no longer be slaves to sin." She testified to an unusual spiritual rest through her new commitment to Christ. Her husband was at first skeptical, but when he had a similar experience, the two of them organized a series of interdenominational meetings aimed at bringing other Christians to this victory over sin by their entrance into "the higher Christian life."

In 1872, the Smiths moved to Britain for Robert's health and continued their meetings there with unusual success. Three years later, Hannah published her highly popular *The Christian's Secret of a Happy Life*. The

Smith meetings led to the founding of the annual Keswick Convention in northern England. The movement later spread to the United States where it continued its emphasis on personal holiness secured through a crisis of surrender to God and spiritual growth by constant trust.

We can detect this dual emphasis—surrender and faith—in the following excerpt from Mrs. Smith's popular book.

LAYING OUR BURDEN DOWN

Most Christians are like a man who was toiling along the road, bending under a heavy burden, when a wagon overtook him, and the driver kindly offered to help him on his journey. He joyfully accepted the offer, but when seated, continued to bend beneath his burden, which he still kept on his shoulders. "Why do you not lay down your burden?" asked the kind-hearted driver. "Oh!" replied the man, "I feel that it is almost too much to ask you to carry me, and I could not think of letting you carry my burden too." And so Christians, who have given themselves into the care and keeping·of the Lord Jesus, still continue to bend beneath the weight of their burden, and often go weary and heavy-laden throughout the whole length of their journey.

When I speak of burdens, I mean everything that troubles us, whether spiritual or temporal.

I mean, first of all, ourselves. The greatest burden we have to carry in life is self. The most difficult thing we have to manage is self. Our own daily living, our frames and feelings, our especial weaknesses and temptations, . . . these are the things that perplex and worry us more than anything else, and that bring us oftenest into bondage and darkness. In laying off your burdens, therefore, the first one you must get rid of is yourself. . . .

Next, you must lay off every other burden,—your health, your reputation, your Christian work, your houses, your children, your business, your servants; everything, in short, that concerns you, whether inward or outward. . . .

I knew a Christian lady who had a very heavy temporal burden. It took away her sleep and her appetite, and there was danger of her health breaking down under it. . . . The circumstances of her life she could not alter, but she took them to the Lord, and handed them over into His management; and then she believed that He took it, and she left all the responsibility and the worry and anxiety with Him. . . . She abandoned her whole self to the Lord, with all that she was and all that she had, and, believing that He took that which she had committed to Him, she ceased to fret and worry, and her life became all sunshine in the gladness of belonging to Him. And this was the Higher Christian Life! . . .

Would you like to get rid of your burdens? Do you not long to hand over the management of your unmanageable self into the hands of One who is able to manage you? Are you not tired and weary, and does not the rest I speak of look sweet to you? . . .

Your part is simply to rest. His part is to sustain you, and He cannot fail.[42]

Part 6

Saints in Modern Times

On Sunday, April 8, 1945, a number of the prisoners in the concentration camp at Flossenburg, Germany, shared a little worship service. While the members of the congregation were of several nationalities, the leader of the service was young German pastor Dietrich Bonhoeffer. He drew his thoughts from Isaiah's text: "With his stripes are we healed." An English officer reported that he spoke in a way that went to everyone's heart.

Bonhoeffer had hardly ended his concluding prayer when the door opened and in came two civilians. They said, "Prisoner Bonhoeffer, come with us." That could mean only one thing for a prisoner, death on the gallows. His fellow prisoners bade him good-by and as he leaned close to one of them, he whispered, "This is the end, but for me it is the beginning of life." The next day he was hanged.

Bonhoeffer was executed because he dared to challenge the Nazi dogma of the Aryan race. He had heard of the secret plans for the overthrow of Hitler and had concluded in his soul that to withdraw from this resistance to the Nazis would be irresponsible cowardice and flight from reality.

THE TIMES

The struggle within Bonhoeffer's soul is typical of Christian discipleship in the twentieth century. While most Christian believers have avoided a clash with unbelief as dramatic as Bonhoeffer's, saints have often had to follow Christ through violent storms spawned by international ideologies. We call them "ideologies" because they are sets of ideas that reflect the aspirations and determine the destinies of masses of people today.

The one nearest most of us is the increasingly secular faith of Western nations, including the United States. It is a faith that draws upon the ideals of the eighteenth-century Englightenment, a way of enjoying life liberated from the demands of traditional Judeo-Christian morality. It believes deeply in the virtues of democratic principles, including the rights of the individual and the certainty of human progress in history. Its gospel is individual "freedoms," freedom to say anything, to see anything, to do anything short of the destruction of civil peace.

"The American Way" or the "principles of the Western world" are not directly hostile to Christianity. The culture is simply disinterested in religion. The spirit of our times was reflected in an episode from the fading life of Henry David Thoreau. A friend tried to turn his mind, in that somber hour of death, to the things of eternity, but Thoreau replied, "One world at a time, brother; one world at a time." Thoreau had discovered an autonomous and independent value in this life and he saw no pressing need to prepare for the next life. His humanistic spirit is shared today by most men and women in Western societies.

The democratic ideology conflicts with another, the Marxist faith of the Communist block nations. Communism has a hypnotic appeal for hosts of people in the twentieth century because it appears to describe life as masses of people acutally encounter it—in oppression, deprivation, and want.

The Communist gospel promises a new future for the poor. It sees history driven by the conflict between those who "have" and those who "have not." This conflict, Communists insist, can only lead to revolution and the overthrow of the oppressors. After the revolution comes a Communist regime, the new ruling elite, who will guarantee land reforms and a new economy, jobs for the poor, education for the young, and pride for the people.

Western nations and the leader of the Communist block, the Soviet Union, allied briefly in the 1940s to beat back the Nazi threat, but recent years have seen the rise of a third ideology that centers in the religious faith of the Arab world. It draws deeply from the five laws of Islam, but is politically inflamed by an intense hatred of Israel and the United States. This faith in a united Arab world is largely negative because it feeds on hostility toward "the Christian West." The growing number of mosques appearing in Western nations, however, testifies to Islam's recent evangelistic mission.

The saints in this, our final section lived through the international tensions of the twentieth century, through World War I, the creation of the Soviet Union, the rise and fall of Naziism in World War II, and the Korean conflict. Through it all, however, they demonstrate the possibility of faith in Christ in "trouble, hardship, persecution, famine, nakedness, danger, and sword."

43

Obedience

ANDREW MURRAY (1828–1917)

N ew Zealand must be a fascinating place. I have never been there, but I understand from those who have that the country is home for more flightless birds than any other country. The kiwi, the kakapo, the penguin, and the weka rail can be found there. These birds all had wings once upon a time but lost them simply by neglecting them. Food was apparently so abundant, and danger so uncommon, that the birds lost the ability to fly. Because they had no necessity to fly, they lost the ability to fly.

Surely the same principle of neglect applies to important powers in the spiritual life. Meditation neglected is soon meditation lost. Compassion neglected is soon compassion lost. In a word, obedience is essential to spiritual vitality. The Christian must respond when the Scriptures command or the Spirit prompts. Otherwise, neglect will destroy the power to act. Andrew Murray, the South African missionary statesman, saw this clearly.

After his education in Scotland and Holland, Murray served in several posts in South Africa. Six times he was elected moderator of the Dutch Reformed Church in the Cape Colony. During the 1860s, he led the fight in his church against theological liberalism and in 1895, addressed the Keswick conference in England and D. L. Moody's Northfield convention in Massachusetts.

Outside of South Africa, however, Christians most likely met Andrew Murray through one of his two hundred and fifty publications. In *With Christ in the School of Prayer,* he shares with his readers "some thoughts on our training for the ministry of intercession." The book circulated widely in Bible schools and homes throughout the English-speaking world in the first half of the twentieth century. The following excerpt is a sample of Murray's power to challenge the democratic faith in the individual by stressing the mandates of Scripture.

THE FATHER'S HOME

There is a danger in our evangelical religion of looking too much at what it offers from one side, as a certain experience to be obtained in prayer and faith. There is another side which God's word puts very strongly, that of obedience as the only path to blessing.

What we need is to realize that in our relationship to the Infinite Being whom we call God, who has created and redeemed us, the first sentiment that ought to animate us is that of subjection. The surrender to His supremacy, His glory, His will, His pleasure, ought to be the first and uppermost thought of life.

The question is not, how we are to obtain and enjoy His favour, for in this the main thing may still be self. But what this Being in the very nature of things rightfully claims, and is infinitely and unspeakably worthy of, is that His glory and pleasure should be my one object. Surrender to His perfect and blessed will, a life of service and obedience, is the beauty and the charm of heaven. Service and obedience, these were the thoughts that were uppermost in the mind of the Son, when He dwelt upon earth. Service and obedience, these must become with us the chief objects of desire and aim, more so than rest or light, or joy or strength. . . .

"If a man love me he will keep my words, and the Father and I will come and take up our abode with him." Could words put it more clearly that obedience is the way to the indwelling of the Spirit, to His revealing the Son within us, and to His again preparing us to be the abode, the home of the Father? The indwelling of the Three-One God is the heritage of them that obey. Obedience and faith are but two aspects of the one act,—surrender to God and His will. As faith strengthens for obedience, it is in turn strengthened by it: faith is made perfect by works.

Those who have made the deaf and dumb their study, tell us how much power of speaking depends on that of hearing, and how the loss of hearing in children is followed by that of speaking too. This is true in a wider sense: as we hear, so we speak. . . .

To offer a prayer—to give utterance to certain wishes and to appeal to certain promises—is an easy thing, and can be learned of man by human wisdom. But to pray in the Spirit, to speak words that reach and touch God, that affect and influence the powers of the unseen world,—such praying, such speaking, depends entirely upon our hearing God's voice. . . .

This hearing the voice of God is something more than the thoughtful study of the Word. There may be a study and knowledge of the Word, in which there is but little real fellowship with the living God. But there is also a reading of the Word, in the very presence of the Father, and under the leading of the Spirit, in which the Word comes to us in the living power from God Himself; it is to us the very voice of the Father, a real personal fellowship with Himself. It is the living voice of God that enters the heart, that brings blessing and strength, and awakens the response of a living faith that reaches the heart of God again.

It is on this hearing the voice, that the power both to obey and believe depends. The chief thing is, not to know what God has said we must do, but that God Himself says it to us. It is not the law, and not the book, not the knowledge of what is right, that works obedience, but the personal influence of God and His living fellowship. . . . It is only in the full presence of God that disobedience and unbelief become impossible.[43]

44

Motives

OSWALD CHAMBERS (1874–1917)

Introspection! Most spiritual guides recognize it for what it is: quicksand across the path to spiritual maturity. It is a danger spot in the Christian life because the distinction between genuine impressions from the Spirit of God and pseudo-impressions created by our own twisted affections is subtle, extremely subtle. Many guides believe that the best course for Christian pilgrims is to avoid introspection altogether. Simply do the right thing, they say, and leave the motives to God.

Many believers in some form of Christian work, however, have followed another path. They have learned how to negotiate their introspection spots— thanks to the help of a special guide, Oswald Chambers.

Chambers is another of those spiritual scouts from Scotland. He was born into a Baptist pastor's home in Aberdeen. He was converted, however, through the ministry of England's best-known preacher during the last quarter of the nineteenth century, Charles Haddon Spurgeon.

Chambers studied in London and at Edinburgh before entering Dunoon College in 1897 to train for the Baptist ministry. During these student days he met William Quarrier, founder of the Orphan Homes in Scotland, and his life was changed. He seems to have entered into a fresh experience of prayer and faith. He decided to join the Pentecostal League of Prayer founded by Reader Harris. He traveled about as an evangelist. Then, from 1911–1915, he served as principal of the Bible Training College of Clapham Common, London. His final ministry came during World War I. He served as a superintendent of the YMCA Huts and speaker to the troops in the desert camps at Zeitoun, Egypt.

For two generations now, thousands upon thousands of Christians have read with profit Oswald Chambers brief talks to the students at the Bible Training School and the troops in the Egyptian desert. Many of his more penetrating observations are in his most popular collection, *My Utmost For His Highest*. Here are two examples of Chamber's insights into Christian motives.

TEMPERAMENTAL CHRISTIANITY

"Building up yourselves on your most holy faith" (Jude 20).

There was nothing either of the nature of impulse or of cold-bloodedness about our Lord, but only a calm strength that never got into panic. Most of us develop our Christianity along the line of our temperament, not along the line of God. Impulse is a trait in natural life, but our Lord always ignores it, because it hinders the development of the life of the disciple. Watch how the Spirit of God checks impulse, His checks bring a rush of self-conscious foolishness which makes us instantly want to vindicate ourselves. Impulse is all right in a child, but it is disastrous in a man or woman; an impulsive man is always a petted man. Impulse has to be trained into intuition by discipline.

Discipleship is built entirely on the supernatural grace of God. Walking on the water is easy to impulsive pluck, but walking on dry land as a disciple of Jesus Christ is a different thing. Peter walked on the water to go to Jesus, but he followed him afar off on the land. We do not need the grace of God to stand crisis, human nature and pride are sufficient, we can face the strain magnificently; but it does require the supernatural grace of God to live twenty-four hours in every day as a saint, to go through the drudgery as a disciple, to live an ordinary, unobserved, ignored existence as a disciple of Jesus. It is inbred in us that we have to do exceptional things for God; but we have not. We have to be exceptional in the ordinary things, to be holy in mean streets, among mean people, and this is not learned in five minutes.

THE SACRAMENTAL LIFE

"Who now rejoice in my sufferings for you, and fill up that which is behind of the afflictions of Christ. . . ." (Colossians 1:24).

The Christian worker has to be a sacramental "go-between," to be so identified with his Lord and the reality of His Redemption that He can continually bring His creating life through him. It is not the strength of one man's personality being superimposed on another, but the real presence of Christ coming through the elements of the worker's life. When we preach the historic facts of the life and death of our Lord as they are conveyed in the New Testament, our words are made sacramental; God uses them on the ground of His Redemption to create in those who listen that which is not created otherwise. If we preach the effects of Redemption in human life instead of the revelation regarding Jesus, the result in those who listen is not the new birth, but refined spiritual culture, and the Spirit of God cannot witness to it because such preaching is in another domain. We have to see that we are in such living sympathy with God that as we proclaim His truth He can create in souls the things which He alone can do.

"What a wonderful personality!" "What a fascinating man!" "Such marvelous insight!" What chance has the Gospel of God through all that? It cannot

get through, because the line of attraction is always the line of appeal. If a man attracts by his personality, his appeal is along that line; if he is identified with the Lord's personality, then the appeal is along the line of what Jesus Christ can do. The danger is to glory in men; Jesus says we are to lift Him up.[44]

45

Life from a Center

THOMAS R. KELLY (1893–1941)

O ur secular society offers few inducements for personal worship or prayer. Noise, bustle, and billboards assault our emotions and crowd our days with thoughts of this moment and this place. Who has time for God?

Thomas R. Kelly was one of the first spiritual guides to recognize the difficulties of keeping the soul alive in a city. Retreat, he said, is not the answer. Drawing upon his Quaker heritage, he urged us to return to the Center of life, the Living Christ within us.

Kelly left his farm home in southwestern Ohio to attend Haverford College, Hartford Theological Seminary, and Harvard University. During 1917–18, he worked with German prisoners in England, and in 1924–25, he led the Quaker community in Berlin, Germany.

After these years of education and service in Europe, he taught at Earlham College in Indiana and spent one year in Hawaii, where he taught at the university and studied oriental philosophy. In 1936, he accepted an invitation to Haverford to replace professor Elton Trueblood in the philosophy department.

Kelly was a popular teacher and often spoke to Quaker meetings. Several of the essays in *A Testament of Devotion* were originally delivered to Quaker gatherings. His untimely death from a heart attack came in January, 1941.

The following excerpts underscore Kelly's concern to live on two levels simultaneously.

THE LIGHT WITHIN

The problem we face today needs very little time for its statement. Our lives in a modern city grow too complex and overcrowded. Even the necessary obligations which we feel we must meet grow overnight, like Jack's beanstalk, and before we know it we are bowed down with burdens, crushed under committees, strained, breathless, and hurried, panting through a never-ending program of appointments. We are too busy to be good wives to our husbands, good homemakers, good companions of our children, good friends to our friends, and with no time at all to be friends to the friendless. But if we withdraw from public engagements and interests, in order to spend quiet hours with the family, the guilty calls of citizenship whisper disquieting claims in our ears. . . .

I would suggest that the true explanation of the complexity of our program is an inner one, not an outer one. The outer distractions of our interests reflect an inner lack of integration of our own lives. We are trying to be several selves at once, without all our selves being organized by a single, mastering Life within us. Each of us tends to be, not a single self, but a whole committee of selves. There is the civic self, the parental self, the financial self, the religious self, the society self, the professional self, the literary self. . . .

Life is meant to be lived from a Center, a divine Center. . . . There is a divine Abyss within us all, a holy infinite Center, a Heart, a Life who speaks in us and through us to the world. We have all heard this holy Whisper at times. At times we have followed the Whisper, and an amazing equilibrium of life, amazing effectiveness of living sets in. But too many of us have heeded the Voice only at times. Only at times have we submitted to His holy guidance. We have not counted this Holy Thing within us to be the most precious thing in the world. We have not surrendered all else, to attend to it alone. . . .

What is here urged are secret habits of unceasing orientation of the deeps of our being about the Inward Light, ways of conducting our inward life so that we are perpetually bowed in worship, while we are also very busy in the world of daily affairs. . . .

There is a way of ordering our mental life on more than one level at once. On one level we may be thinking, discussing, seeing, calculating, meeting all the demands of external affairs. But deep within, behind the scenes, at a profounder level, we may also be in prayer and adoration, song and worship and a gentle receptiveness to divine breathings.

The secular world today values and cultivates only the first level, assured that there is where the real business of mankind is done, and scorns, or smiles in tolerant amusement, at the cultivation of the second level—a luxury enterprise, a vestige of superstition, an occupation for special temperaments. But in a deeply religious culture men know that the deep level of prayer and of divine attendance is the most important thing in the world. It is at this deep level that the real business of life is determined.[45]

46

Fellowship with God

WILLIAM TEMPLE (1881–1944)

W. E. Sangster used to say that it is important to "get the 'me' into the Cross." He had in mind, among other examples, Martin Luther, who said in his commentary on Galatians, "Read . . . with great vehemency these words *'me* and for *me'*, and so inwardly practice with thyself, that thou, with a sure faith, mayst conceive and print this 'me' in thy heart, and apply it to thyself, not doubting that thou art of the number of those to whom this 'me' belongeth."

The evangelical tradition has, since Luther's day, linked true spirituality with Bible study that "gets the 'me' into the Cross." The practice arose, no doubt, from the conviction that God had spoken to man uniquely in the Scriptures. So the primary way to deepen fellowship with God was to listen humbly to the Word of God and to live according to its truths.

This conviction, at the heart of evangelical piety, explains the movement's enormous expenditure of energy devoted to the study of the Bible and the writing of commentaries setting forth its meaning. Such study is more than determining the what and where of the original authors; it is also discerning the timeless message of the Scriptures—catching their significance for our lives today.

In the rapidly changing world of the twentieth century, many Christians considered William Temple a dependable guide through the morass created by the competing ideologies. He had many gifts, not the least of which was his knowledge of the Scriptures.

Temple received his education at Rugby and Balliol College, Oxford. From 1904 to 1910 he taught philosophy at Queen's College, Oxford, and then for a decade served as chaplain to the Archbishop of Canterbury and the King of England. His rise to the highest office in the Anglican Church began when he was consecrated Bishop of Manchester (1921–1928). Next came his ministry as Archbishop of York (1928–1942); and, finally, his elevation to the highest post in his church, the Archbishop of Canterbury.

Through all these years Temple revealed a deep concern for social righteousness. He set forth his views on Christianity's place in modern societies in two influential books: *Nature, Man, and God* and *Christianity and Social Order*. Temple balanced his social concern, however, with his commitment to the spiritual life. We can catch a glimpse of his emphasis on the spiritual life and the place of Bible study in it by turning to the pages of his *Readings in St. John's Gospel*. Here is one striking example in which he takes a fresh approach to a familiar passage.

RESTING-PLACES

"Let not your hearts be troubled; believe in God, and believe in me. In my Father's house are many resting-places. If it were not so, should I have told you that I go to prepare a place for you? And if I go and prepare a place for you, I come again and will receive you to myself, that where I am ye also may be."

One who faces his own failures is steadily advancing on the pilgrim's way; he, like his Master, is going to the Father. More than this; if he is thus traveling the right way at all, he is at home with the Father all the time. . . .

The resting-places (Monai) are wayside caravanserais—shelters at stages along the road where travelers may rest on their journey. It was the custom in the East . . . for travelers to send a dragoman [an interpreter or guide] forward to make preparation in the next of those resting-places along the road, so that when they came they might find in it comfort as well as shelter. Here the Lord presents Himself as our spiritual dragoman, who treads the way of faith before us . . . and makes ready to welcome us. It may be that we are still far from perfect fellowship with the Father; like Peter, we are about to deny our Lord, or like the rest, we are about to forsake him in flight. We have a long journey of many days before us ere our pilgrimage is accomplished. But there are, by God's mercy, many resting-places. . . .

The Lord calls us to absolute perfection; but He points us here and now to what is for each one the next stage, the next resting-place, on the way to it. And as we follow, we find Him there to welcome us. More than that—He comes to lead us there. . . . Our spiritual dragoman, who has gone forward to make preparation, returns to encourage us and lead us to the resting-place prepared. That resting-place is fellowship, fuller than before, with the Lord— that where I am ye also may be—until the last stage is reached, towards which we press on, "the goal of the call upward which God gives in Christ Jesus" (Philippians 3:14).

Every Christian must know something of what is here described. We reach a certain stage of fellowship with Christ, in spiritual apprehension and moral attainment, and find great joy in it. But this seems to fade, until we become conscious that we are called to something higher. The Lord is gone before us to prepare the next resting-place. Then everything depends upon our response. We may stay where we are, becoming more and more torpid in spirit. Or we may, in St. Paul's phrase, "press on." If we do this, we find the Lord meeting us and leading us to the next resting-place. Our sense of fellowship with Him revives, and with this our joy in it. Then the process is repeated. So we make progress, "from glory to glory" (2 Corinthians 3:18) till we are "transformed into the same image."[46]

47

Unity in Christ

DIETRICH BONHOEFFER (1906–1945)

O ne of the ever-present dangers of devout souls is unrealistic expecta-
tions, of others and themselves. Life in the spirit tends to make us
impatient with life in the flesh. That is probably why the monastic orders found
it necessary to adopt some rule, some guidelines, for their life together. The
ideal of personal holiness had to be reconciled with the reality of life in
community.

The problem appears today in zealous believers who grow impatient with
"dead" and impersonal churches. Are there any biblical principles for shaping
our life in the Christian community? And can we be content with these?
Dietrich Bonhoeffer tried to answer these questions and others in a helpful
little book he wrote while hiding from the Nazis.

Though growing up with an agnostic father in eastern Germany,
Bonhoeffer became a Lutheran pastor. In 1933, however, Hitler's rise to
power interrupted his career. Two days after Hitler became Chancellor of
Germany, Bonhoeffer dared to oppose the Nazis in a radio speech. He chided
the German people for their hankering for a "leader" who would inevitably
become their "misleader." The broadcast was cut off before Bonhoeffer could
finish.

When the "leader" consolidated his power in Germany, Bonhoeffer spent
two years in exile, serving a Lutheran congregation in London. He returned to
Germany in 1935 to accept an invitation to lead a small "illegal" theological
seminary for the churches which resisted Hitler's authority. *Life Together*
came from this ministry before the Nazi authorities closed the school.

In 1939, while responding to what he felt to be his Christian duty,
Bonhoeffer joined the resistance movement and participated in a plot to
assassinate Hitler. The Gestapo, however, arrested him, and after two years in
concentration camps, Bonhoeffer, on April 9, 1945, was hanged. His life,
writings, and death have placed him among the most influential Christians in
the twentieth century.

Here is Bonhoeffer's reminder for the basis of all genuinely Christian
fellowship.

SHATTERING A WISH DREAM

Innumerable times a whole Christian community has broken down because it had sprung up from a wish dream. The serious Christian, set down for the first time in a Christian community, is likely to bring with him a very definite idea of what Christian life together should be and to try to realize it. But God's grace speedily shatters such dreams. Just as surely as God desires to lead us to a knowledge of genuine Christian fellowship, so surely must we be overwhelmed by a great disillusionment with others, with Christians in general, and, if we are fortunate, with ourselves.

By sheer grace, God will not permit us to live even for a brief period in a dream world. He does not abandon us to those rapturous experiences and lofty moods that come over us like a dream. God is not a God of the emotions but the God of truth. Only that fellowship which faces such disillusionment, with all its unhappy and ugly aspects, begins to be what it should be in God's sight, begins to grasp in faith the promise that is given to it. . . .

God hates visionary dreaming; it makes the dreamer proud and pretentious. The man who fashions a visionary ideal of community demands that it be realized by God, by others, and by himself. He enters the community of Christians with his demands, sets up his own law, and judges the brethren and God Himself accordingly. He stands adamant, a living reproach to all others in the circle of the brethren. He acts as if he is the creator of the Christian community, as if his dream binds men together. When things do not go his way, he calls the effort a failure. When his ideal picture is destroyed, he sees the community going to smash. So he becomes, first an accuser of his brethren, then an accuser of God, and finally the despairing accuser of himself.

Because God has already laid the only foundation of our fellowship, because God has bound us together in one body with other Christians in Jesus Christ, long before we entered into common life with them, we enter into that common life not as demanders but as thankful recipients. We thank God for giving us brethren who live by His call, by His forgiveness, and His promise. We do not complain of what God does not give us; we rather thank God for what He does give us daily. . . .

Only he who gives thanks for little things receives the big things. We prevent God from giving us the great spiritual gifts He has in store for us, because we do not give thanks for daily gifts. We think we dare not be satisfied with the small measure of spiritual knowledge, experience, and love that has been given to us, and that we must constantly be looking forward eagerly for the highest good. Then we deplore the fact that we lack the deep certainty, the strong faith, and the rich experience that God has given to others, and we consider this lament to be pious. We pray for the big things and forget to give thanks for the ordinary, small (and yet really not small) gifts. How can God entrust great things to one who will not thankfully receive from Him the little things? . . .

Christian brotherhood is not an ideal which we must realize; it is rather a reality created by God in Christ in which we may participate. The more clearly we learn to realize that the ground and strength and promise of all our fellowship is in Jesus Christ alone, the more serenely shall we think of our fellowship and pray and hope for it.[47]

48

The Crucified Life

WATCHMAN NEE (1903–1972)

A kindly, elderly grandmother with a handful of pictures of her grandchildren can bore you for an hour with them, but, if you take from your pocket a snapshot or two of your own, she is wearied in a matter of seconds. Why is this?

All the saints know that the thing that is deeply wrong with human nature is not that some people commit adultery and others steal, but that all of us are profoundly self-centered. Manners, education, style and age can cover the disease for a time, but they can't remove the deadly cancer underneath.

Desperate conditions demand radical cures. That is why the saints have spoken so often of the "crucifixion" of the self as the prelude to the "resurrection" to new life in Christ. The metaphor, central to the message of the Keswick conferences, spread throughout evangelical Christianity in the twentieth century, in large part through the writings of a Chinese evangelist named Watchman Nee.

"Watchman" was not his original name. He was born Nee Shu-Tsu, but when his mission in life became evident his mother proposed a name change to Nee To-Sheng, "the sound of a gong." The new name would remind others that a "bell ringer" or Watchman had come to the people of God. And so it proved.

Watchman's Christian parents saw that he received a Western-Christian education, including Trinity College in Foochow. For a time their concern seemed to be misdirected, but in 1920, during a revival at a Methodist Chapel, his mother came under deep conviction of sin. Her confession to Watchman of wrongfully accusing him of a misdeed led Watchman himself to receive the Lord Jesus Christ as his personal Savior.

Through a British missionary in Shanghai, Miss M. E. Barber, Watchman came into contact with the Keswick concept of the victorious Christian life and the books of the Plymouth Brethren. Both had major impact upon his thinking and his ministry.

Soon he gave himself to the work of God among his people. He became one of China's most effective evangelical leaders. Widely known as a gifted preacher, he was probably responsible for establishing more than 200 churches. The movement came to be called the Little Flock.

During and shortly after a visit to Europe in 1938–39, Nee gave a series of messages from the Book of Romans that became the basis for *The Normal Christian Life*. It is probably his best book. By stressing the cross, he avoids some of his later questionable doctrines about the soul and the church.

On October 1, 1949, after overthrowing Chiang Kai-shek, Mao Tse-tung declared the establishment of the People's Republic of China. In September, 1951 the communists launched their accusation meetings against the Little Flock, and in April, 1952 Nee was arrested and began twenty years of confinement. He died on June 1, 1972, but the continued widespread popularity of his books make him, even today, one of the most influential Christians from the Third World during this age of ideologies.

Here is Nee's explanation of the personal experience of the Cross.

VICTORY THROUGH DEFEAT

Why do you believe that the Lord Jesus died? What is your ground for the belief? Is it that you feel He has died? No, you never felt it. You believe it because the Word of God tells you so. When the Lord was crucified, two thieves were crucified at the same time. You do not doubt that they were crucified at the same time. You do not doubt that they were crucified with Him either, because the Scripture says so quite plainly.

You believe in the death of the Lord Jesus and you believe in the death of the thieves with Him. Now what about your own death? Your crucifixion is more intimate than theirs. They were crucified at the same time as the Lord but on different crosses, whereas you were crucified on the selfsame cross as He, for you were in Him when He died. How can you know? You can know for the one sufficient reason that God said so. It does not depend on your feelings. If you feel that Christ has died, He has died; and if you do not feel that He has died, He has died. If you feel that you have died, you have died; and if you do not feel that you have died, you have nevertheless just as surely died. These are divine facts. That Christ has died is a fact, that the two thieves have died is a fact, and that you have died is a fact also. Let me tell you, You have died! You are done with! You are ruled out! The self you loathe is on the Cross of Christ. And "he that is dead is freed from sin" (Romans 6:7 Amplified). This is the Gospel for Christians.

Our crucifixion can never be made effective by will or by effort, but only by accepting what the Lord Jesus did on the Cross. Our eyes must be opened to see the finished work of Calvary. Some of you, prior to your salvation, may have tried to save yourselves. You read the Bible, prayed, went to church, gave alms. Then one day your eyes were opened and you saw that a full salvation had already been provided for you on the Cross. You just accepted that and thanked God, and peace and joy flowed into your heart. And now the good news is that sanctification is made possible for you on exactly the same basis as that initial salvation. You are offered deliverance from sin as no less a gift of God's grace than was the forgiveness of your sins.

For God's way of deliverance is altogether different from man's way. Man's way is to try to suppress sin by seeking to overcome it; God's way is to remove the sinner. Many Christians mourn over their weakness, thinking that if only they were stronger all would be well. The idea that, because failure to lead a holy life is due to our impotence, something more is therefore demanded of us, leads naturally to this false conception of the way of deliverance. If we are preoccupied with the power of sin and with our inability to meet it, then we naturally conclude that to gain the victory over sin we must have more power. "If only I were stronger," we say, "I could overcome my violent outbursts of temper," and so we plead with the Lord to strengthen us that we may exercise more self-control.

But this is altogether a fallacy; it is not Christianity. God's means of delivering us from sin is not by making us stronger and stronger, but by making us weaker and weaker. That is surely rather a peculiar way of victory, you say; but it is the divine way. God sets us free from the dominion of sin, not by strengthening our old man but by crucifying him; not by helping him to do anything, but by removing him from the scene of action.

For years, maybe, you have tried fruitlessly to exercise control over yourself, and perhaps this is still your experience; but when once you see the truth you will recognize that you are indeed powerless to do anything, but that in setting you aside altogether God has done it all. Such discovery brings human striving and self-effort to an end.[48]

49
Prayer

JOHN BAILLIE (1886–1960)

P rayer," John Bunyan once said, "is a sincere, sensible, affectionate pouring out of the soul to God, through Christ in the strength and assistance of the Spirit, for such things as God has promised." Prayer, then, is more than our yearning for some personal benefit. It is our thoughtful and heartfelt response to a God who has already extended his hand of kindness to us.

Some spiritual advisors recommend the repetition of certain forms of prayer. Others insist upon personal, extemporaneous prayers. But almost all of them agree that prayer, in whatever form, is basic to any real progress in our spiritual development.

When the disciples asked Jesus to teach them to pray, he gave them a model, what we call "the Lord's Prayer." In more recent times, many Christians have found additional help in the prayers of John Baillie.

Baillie was a Scottish theologian deeply concerned about the doubts that twentieth-century people felt about the Christian faith. As professor of divinity at the University of Edinburgh, he addressed these doubts. In his popular *And the Life Everlasting,* he defended the Christian view of eternal life. And in his *A Diary of Private Prayer,* he took his readers into his private world of prayer. We have reproduced here one of his morning prayers and one of his evening ones as models of heartfelt and thoughtful intercession.

MORNING!

O God who art from eternity unto eternity, and art not at one time in one place because all times and places are in Thee, I would now seek to understand my destiny as a child of Thine. Here I stand, weak and mortal, amid the immensities of nature. But blessed be Thou, O Lord God, that Thou hast made me in Thine own likeness and hast breathed into me the breath of Thine own life. Within this poor body Thou hast set a spirit that is akin to Thine own Spirit. Within this corruptible Thou hast planted incorruption and within this mortal immortality. So from this little room and this short hour I can lift up my mind beyond all time and space to Thee, the uncreated One, until the light of Thy countenance illumines all my life.

Let me keep in mind that my mortal body is but the servant of my immortal soul:

Let me keep in mind how uncertain is my hold upon my bodily life:

Let me remember that here I have no continuing city, but only a place of sojourn and a time of testing and of training:

Let me use this world as not abusing it:

Let me be in this world but not of it:

Let me be as having nothing yet possessing all things:

Let me understand the vanity of the temporal and the glory of the eternal:

Let my world be centered not in myself but in Thee:

Almighty God, who didst raise from the dead our Lord Jesus Christ and didst set Him at Thy right hand in glory everlasting, I thank Thee for this hope of immortality with which through many ages Thou hast cheered and enlightened the souls of Thy saints, and which Thou didst most surely seal through the same Jesus Christ our Lord. Amen.

AND EVENING

Almighty God, in this hour of quiet I seek communion with Thee. From the fret and fever of the day's business, from the world's discordant noises, from the praise and blame of men, from the confused thoughts and vain imaginations of my own heart, I would now turn aside and seek the quietness of Thy presence. All day long I have toiled and striven; but now, in stillness of heart and in the clear light of Thine eternity, I would ponder the pattern my life has been weaving.

May there fall upon me now, O God, a great sense of Thy power and Thy glory, so that I may see all earthly things in their true measure.

Let me not be ignorant of this great thing, that one day is with Thee as a thousand years and a thousand years as one day.

Give me now such understanding of Thy perfect holiness as will make an end of all pride in my own attainment.

Grant unto me now such a vision of Thine uncreated beauty as will make me dissatisfied with all lesser beauties.

Though earth and man were gone,
And suns and universes cease to be,
And Thou wert left alone,
Every existence would exist in Thee.

I am content, O Father, to leave my life in Thy hands, believing that the very hairs upon my head are numbered by Thee. I am content to give over my will to Thy control, believing that I can find in Thee a righteousness that I could never have won for myself. I am content to leave all my dear ones to Thy care, believing that Thy love for them is greater than my own. I am content to leave in Thy hands the causes of truth and justice, and the coming of Thy Kingdom in the hearts of men, believing that my ardour for them is but a feeble shadow of Thy purpose. To Thee, O God, be glory for ever. Amen.[49]

50

New Creatures

W. E. SANGSTER (1900–1960)

C hrist enlarges our capacity for friendship. He increases our love, turns our generous thoughts out upon others, makes us unconsciously more attractive, and adds charm that does not belong to nature alone. The Greek word *charis* which is translated in the New Testament as 'grace' also means 'charm.' The grace of the Lord Jesus Christ adds charm to unlovely sinners. It lights them up from the inside. . . . Our bias to believe the worst of people has been turned into a bias to believe the best."

The man who said this believed in holiness. And you can't ask for a much better description. It came from W. E. Sangster, the popular Methodist preacher and scholar in London during the 1940s and 50s.

Sangster grew up in London and was educated at Richmond College, Surrey. He saw military service during World War I and in 1926 was ordained into the Methodist ministry. He ministered in several English towns, including Liverpool and Leeds, before returning to London to serve the Central Hall, Westminster, where his magnetic preaching attracted large crowds. He was President of the London Free Church Federation (1944–1946) and President of the Methodist Conference (1950).

Sangster knew John Wesley well and considered himself a follower of the great revivalist and his doctrine of holiness. His doctoral dissertation, published as *The Path to Perfection*, was a study of John Wesley's doctrine.

Sangster, however, was more than a scholar. His passion was preaching. He shared his philosophy of communicating the Gospel in his *The Craft of a Sermon*. But those who heard him once could not forget him. One correspondent in the *Church of England Newspaper* recalled Sangster's impact on him. "As I sat spellbound, listening to him, I felt an overwhelming impression . . . that I was listening to a man speaking from another world, to a visitant from some other sphere."

In the two excerpts that follow, Sangster underscores the new life generated by personal holiness.

STRANGE DIGNITY

The real you is the self which Christ could make you. You were not made to grovel. You were not built to abide in sin. God made you for Himself, and deep-set in your heart there are longings for holiness, and every now and then the Spirit inflames them and you long for the great spaces in which the saint moves.

I was in the Zoo some time ago and lingered by the cages of the eagles. Somehow or other the sight of them hurt me. I looked at the great wing-spread of the King of Birds, and felt sick at heart that they were caged. . . . Made for the skies . . . and crammed in a cage.

So many of us are like that; made for the skies and imprisoned in sin. When Jesus looks at us, He sees us as we are, but, with His double vision, He sees us also as we might be.

He looked on Simon and saw Peter. He looked on Saul and saw Paul. He looked on Augustine the roue, and saw Augustine the saint. . . . If only we could see ourselves as Christ sees us! If we could stand at His elbow and get that double vision; the men and women we are; the men and women we might be! . . . See yourself then 'the man God meant.' Hold the picture in the eye of relevant imagination whenever you pray. Dwell (on your knees) on the thought that God could make you like that . . . and, as you dwell on it daily and in prayer, God will use your sanctified imagination to pull you up. The actual will turn into the ideal. The difference may be so marked that you will need a new name. To you, as to one long ago, He may say "Thou art Simon . . . Thou shalt be called 'Rock.' "

There is nothing dignified about a donkey. You can look at him from any angle you like and you will fail to find what men call "presence." He hasn't got it. He is awkward, obstinate, and, some have thought, a stupid beast. It is the presence of the donkey which makes Christ's triumphal march the most peculiar thing of its kind in history. Whoever heard of a conqueror riding in triumph on an ass? If any Gentiles had been present when the procession passed by, they must have been quietly amused. To give a common donkey a prominent position was enough to take the dignity out of any demonstration. . . . Not that it appeared in that light to the Jews! . . . The Jews' ideal man was a man of peace, and when the Messiah came he would come in the accouterments of peace; not on a prancing steed and with the blare of trumpets, but meekly, riding upon an ass.

And, as I have been looking again into that curious processional scene, I feel somehow that the donkey didn't let it all down. So far from dragging the lowly pomp down to his level, he seems rather to have been drawn up to its. He has caught a strange dignity and quiet consciousness of privilege. The scene is not ludicrous but royal. The awkward, obstinate and despised beast, has been chosen by the Son of God, and he seems aware of his elevation. . . . And I see a parable in that. Whatever Christ touched He dignified, and no matter how despised a person or creature may be, Christ has a use for him. Let me say that again. No matter how ordinary, ill-educated, disfigured, ill-born, one-talented or obscure a man or woman may be, Christ has a use for them, and He gives them dignity by that use.[50]

51
Trough Periods

C. S. LEWIS (1898–1963)

Years ago, Christians really believed that they faced an adversary on their spiritual journey. The hermits in the Egyptian deserts believed it; Martin Luther, in his room at the Wartburg, believed it; and John Bunyan, in his description of Pilgrim's perils, clearly believed it. Today we are less sure. "Isn't the Devil a myth of our prescientific past? Today we have psychological and sociological explanations for our inner conflicts." At least one recent author, C. S. Lewis, dared to challenge these ideas.

The atheist philosopher C. M. Joad once said that C. S. Lewis possessed the "rare gift of making righteousness readable." British people discovered this first during World War II when Lewis delivered a series of twenty-nine popular broadcasts about basic Christian doctrine and then published them under the title *Mere Christianity*. Today, through his books, Lewis probably instructs more people in the basics of Christianity than all the theological faculties in the world.

Lewis was raised an Anglican, but during his teen years, under the influence of a tutor, he became an atheist. Military service during World War I interrupted his education at Oxford. He returned to the university only after recovering from a shell wound. During the 1920s, Lewis moved slowly away from his atheism and returned to the Christian faith and worship in the Church of England, "the most dejected and reluctant convert in history."

In 1954, after nearly thirty years as fellow of Magdalen College at Oxford, Lewis moved to Cambridge and a newly created chair of Medieval and Renaissance English. Through all these years, Lewis released a steady stream of books, which covered a wide range of material, including novels, children's books, theology, poetry, and literary criticism.

One of Lewis's most popular works was a clever satire, written in 1941, called *Screwtape Letters,* a series of instructions from a senior devil, Screwtape, to a junior devil, Wormwood, about how to snatch a new Christian from the snares of heaven. Here is one of the letters.

UNDULATIONS OF THE SOUL

My Dear Wormwood,
So you "have great hopes that the patient's religious phase is dying away,"
have you? . . . Has no one ever told you about the law of Undulation? . . .
Humans are amphibians—half spirit and half animal. . . . As spirits they
belong to the eternal world, but as animals they inhabit time. This means that
while their spirits can be directed to an eternal object, their bodies, passions,
and imaginations are in continual change, for to be in time means to change.
Their nearest approach to constancy, therefore, is undulation—the repeated
return to a level from which they repeatedly fall back, a series of troughs and
peaks. . . . The dryness and dulness through which your patient is now going
are not, as you fondly suppose, your workmanship; they are merely a natural
phenomenon which will do us no good unless you make a good use of it.
To decide what the best use of it is, you must ask what use the Enemy wants to
make of it, and then do the opposite. Now it may surprise you to learn that in
His efforts to get permanent possession of a soul, He relies on the troughs
even more than on the peaks; some of His special favorites have gone through
longer and deeper troughs than anyone else. . . . One must face the fact that
all the talk about His love for men, and His service being perfect freedom, is
not . . . mere propaganda, but an appalling truth. He really does want to fill
the universe with a lot of loathsome little replicas of Himself—creatures
whose life, on its miniature scale, will be qualitatively like His own, not
because He has absorbed them but because their wills freely conform to
His. . . .
And that is where the troughs come in. You must have often wondered why the
Enemy does not make more use of His power to be sensibly present to human
souls in any degree He chooses and at any moment. But you see that the
Irresistible and the Indisputable are the two weapons which the very nature of
His scheme forbids Him to use. Merely to over-ride a human will . . . would be
for Him useless. He cannot ravish. He can only woo. For His ignoble idea is
to eat the cake and have it; the creatures are to be one with Him, but yet
themselves; merely to cancel them, or assimilate them, will not serve. He is
prepared to do a little over-riding at the beginning. He will set them off with
some communications of His Presence which, though faint, seem great to
them, with emotional sweetness, and easy conquest over temptation. But He
never allows this state of affairs to last long. Sooner or later He withdraws, if
not in fact, at least from their conscious experience, all those supports and
incentives. He leaves the creature to stand on its own two legs—to carry out
from the will alone duties which have lost all relish. It is during such trough
periods, much more than during peak periods, that it is growing into the sort
of creature He wants it to be. . . .
But of course the troughs afford opportunities to our side also. Next week I
will give you some hints on how to exploit them.

Your affectionate uncle,
Screwtape[51]

52

Spiritual Receptivity

A. W. TOZER (1897–1963)

W hy do a few Christians seem to be in touch with God personally while the rest of us go through our religious duties like so many Sunday-morning zombies? Are there special creatures called "saints"—and we know we are not among them—or are we too busy or unwilling to pay the price of regular contact with the eternal world?

One twentieth-century American Christian dared to raise that question and offer a disturbing answer. I am thinking of A. W. Tozer.

Tozer once said that the best book is the one that makes you want to put it down and think for yourself. That is the way he wrote, and it made him one of the more widely-read American evangelicals in the twentieth century.

Aiden Wilson Tozer was born in Newburg, Pennsylvania, but in 1912, his family moved from their farm to Akron, Ohio. Three years later, Tozer confessed Christ as his personal Savior and plunged into a life of devotional intensity. In 1919, he entered the ministry when he accepted the call to a Christian and Missionary Alliance church at Nutter Fort, West Virginia. Later he served churches in Morgantown, West Virginia; Toledo, Ohio; and Indianapolis, Indiana.

In 1928, Tozer moved to the Southside Alliance Church in Chicago, where he remained for thirty-one years. He reached far beyond his own congregation, however, through his writings. In May 1950, he agreed to edit *The Alliance Weekly* (later renamed *The Alliance Witness*) and turned its editorials into his pulpit-in-print.

In a materialistic society, Tozer was an evangelical mystic. As one admirer put it, he urged his readers "to please God and forget the crowd." His most popular book, and the one in which his passion glows, is *The Pursuit of God*.

Late in 1959, Tozer left Chicago to become the pastor of the Avenue Road Church in Toronto, Canada. On May 12, 1963, a sudden heart attack ended his ministry and his "pursuit."

In the following excerpt, Tozer puts his finger on the pulse of all genuine spirituality, the heartbeat for God.

ONE CELEBRATED FACT

What does the divine immanence mean in direct Christian experience? It means simply that God is here. Wherever we are, God is here. There is no place, there can be no place, where He is not. . . .

If God is present at every point in space, if we cannot go where He is not, . . . why then has not that Presence become the one universally celebrated fact of the world? The patriarch Jacob, "in the waste howling wilderness," gave the answer to that question. He saw a vision of God and cried out in wonder, "Surely the Lord is in this place; and I knew it not."

The Presence and the manifestation of the Presence are not the same. There can be the one without the other. God is here when we are wholly unaware of it. He is manifest only when and as we are aware of His Presence. . . .

Pick at random a score of great saints whose lives and testimonies are widely known. Let them be Bible characters or well known Christians of post-Biblical times. You will be struck instantly with the fact that the saints were not alike. . . . The differences are as wide as human life itself. . . . Yet they all walked, each in his day, upon a high road of spiritual living far above the common way.

Their differences must have been incidental and in the eyes of God of no significance. In some vital quality they must have been alike. What was it?

I venture to suggest that the one vital quality which they had in common was spiritual receptivity. Something in them was open to heaven, something urged them Godward. . . .

Receptivity is not a single thing; it is a compound rather, a blending of several elements within the soul. It is an affinity for, a bent toward, a sympathetic response to, a desire to have. . . . It may be increased by exercise or destroyed by neglect. It is not a sovereign and irresistible force which comes upon us as a seizure from above. It is a gift of God, indeed, but one which must be recognized and cultivated as any other gift if it is to realize the purpose for which it was given. . . .

The idea of cultivation and exercise, so dear to the saint of old, has now no place in our total religious picture. It is too slow, too common. We now demand glamour and fast flowing dramatic action. . . . To put it differently, we have accepted one another's notions, copied one another's lives and made one another's experiences the model of our own. . . .

It will require a determined heart and more than a little courage to wrench ourselves loose from the grip of our times and return to Biblical ways. But it can be done. . . .

Let any man turn to God in earnest, let him begin to exercise himself unto godliness, let him seek to develop his powers of spiritual receptivity by trust and obedience and humility, and the results will exceed anything he may have hoped in his leaner and weaker days.[52]

FOR FURTHER READING

For readers who want to follow the guidance of some saint beyond the pages of this book, help is readily available. Joseph D. Allison has written *The Devotional Resource Guide* (Nashville: Thomas Nelson Publishers, 1986). It has extensive annotated bibliographies on eleven types of devotional reading and can lead the reader to books, publishers, and editions of hundreds of selections.

In addition, several publishers are currently engaged in issuing sets of spiritual classics. These include the *Classics of Faith and Devotion* from Multnomah Press, the *Classics of Western Spirituality* from Paulist Press, and a steady stream of such literature from The Upper Room in Nashville, Tennessee, perhaps the world's largest publisher of devotional literature. The little set from The Upper Room called *Great Devotional Classics* is especially helpful. It consists of 26 small booklets of selections from the classics, convenient for carrying in a pocket or purse.

Notes

[1] Romans 8:28–39 (NIV).

[2] Cyril C. Richardson, trans. and ed., *Early Christian Fathers* 1 (Philadelphia: Westminster Press, 1953), 213–214.

[3] Ibid., 151–54, 156.

[4] Alexander Roberts and James Donaldson, eds., *The Ante-Nicene Fathers* 5 (Buffalo, New York: Christian Literature Co., 1886), 402–404.

[5] G. W. Butterworth, trans., *On First Principles* 2 (Gloucester, Maine: Peter Smith, 1973), vi, 2. (I have created shorter paragraphs and updated a few spellings to improve readability.)

[6] Herbert Musurillo, S. J., trans., *From Glory to Glory: Texts from Gregory of Nyssa's Mystical Writings* (Crestwood, New York: St. Vladimir's Seminary Press, 1979), 98–102.

[7] Sherwood Eliot Wirt, trans., *Love Song* (New York: Harper & Row, 1971), 124–128.

[8] David A. Fleming, S.M., ed., *The Fire and the Cloud* (Mahwah, New Jersey: Paulist Press, 1978), 65–67.

[9] James M. Houston, ed., *The Love of God* (Portland, Oregon: Multnomah Press, 1983), 188–192.

[10] Raphael Brown, *The Little Flowers of St. Francis of Assisi* (New York: Doubleday, 1958.

[11] Bengt Hoffman, trans., *The Theologia Germanica of Martin Luther* (Mahwah, New Jersey: Paulist Press, 1980), 72–74.

[12] Thomas à Kempis, *Imitation of Christ* (Chicago: M.A. Donohue, n.d.), 1–6, 50–52, 44–45. (In the interest of readability, I have taken the liberty to create paragraphs along contemporary lines.)

[13] Theodore G. Tappert, trans., *Luther: Letters of Spiritual Counsel* 18 (Philadelphia: Westminster Press, 1955), 4–65, 96–97.

[14] George Huston Williams and Angel M. Mergal, eds., *Spiritual and Anabaptist Writers* 20 (Philadelphia: Westminster Press, 1957), 138–144.

[15] Ford Lewis Battle John Calvin's *The Piety of John Calvin* (Grand Rapids, Michigan: Baker, 1978), 54–55. ("On the Christian Life" was originally chapter 17 of the 1539 edition of the *Institutes*.)

[16] Peter C. Erb, trans., *True Christianity* (Mahwah, New Jersey: Paulist Press, 1979), 110–115.

[17] Kieran Kavanaugh and Otilio Rodriguez, trans., *The Interior Castle* (Mahwah, New Jersey: Paulist Press, 1979), 91–94.

[18] John K. Ryan, ed. and trans., *Introduction to the Devout Life* (New York: Harper & Brothers, 1950), 42–44.

[19] *The Book of Common Prayer* (New York: Thomas Nelson & Sons, 1896).

[20] Thomas S. Kepler, ed., *The Private Devotions of Lancelot Andrewes* (World, 1956), 97–101.

[21] John N. Wall, Jr., ed., *The Country Parson, The Temple* (Mahwah, New Jersey: Paulist Press, 1981), 113–114. (I have taken the liberty to provide a few paragraphs for readability.)

[22]W. F. Trotter, trans., *Pensèes* (New York: Modern Library, 1941), 38, 80–83 and 182.

[23]Jeremy Taylor, *The Rules and Exercises of Holy Living* (n.p.: Derby and Jackson, 1859), 126–146.

[24]Winthrop S. Hudson, ed., *The Life of God in the Soul of Man* (Philadelphia: Westminster Press, 1948), 37, 69–88.

[25]John Bunyan's *Pilgrim's Progress* (Grand Rapids, Michigan: Zondervan Publishing House, 1967), Part One.

[26]John Flavel, *The Method of Grace* (Grand Rapids, Michigan: Baker, 1977), 470–481.

[27]E. M. Blaiklock, trans., *The Practice of the Presence of God* (Nashville, Tennessee: Thomas Nelson, 1981), 28–31.

[28]Richard Baxter, *The Saints' Everlasting Rest,* Benjamin Fawcett's abridged ed.(n.p.: American Tract Society, n.d.), 333–353.

[29]Peter C. Erb, ed., *Pietists' Selected Writings* (Mahwah, New Jersey: Paulist Press, 1983), 76–80.

[30]François Fenelon, *Christian Perfection* (New York: Harper, 1947), 82–85.

[31]Elizabeth Rowe, *Devout Exercises of the Heart* (n.p.: Publishing House of the M. E. Church, South, 1893), 22–28.

[32]Philip Doddridge, *Rise and Progress of Religion in the Soul,* Chapter 27. (We have shortened some of the paragraphs for improved readability.)

[33]Jonathan Edwards, *The Works of President Edwards* vol. 1 (n.p.: Leavitt & Co., 1851), 16, 18, 20–22. (I have provided a few paragraphs for readability.)

[34]David Brainerd's *Journal,* Chapter 7.

[35]Philips P. Moulton, ed., *The Journal and Major Essays of John Woolman* (New York: Oxford University Press, 1971).

[36]John Wesley, *The Works of John Wesley,* vol. 6, (Grand Rapids, Michigan: Zondervan, n. d.), 65–77. (His convictions about the world as his parish came in a letter to James Hervey from London, dated March 20, 1739. Albert C. Outler, ed., *Library of Protestant Thought* (New York: Oxford University Press, 1964), 70–73.)

[37]Hannah More, *Strictures on the Modern System of Female Education* 2 vols. (London: T. Cadell, 1799), Chapter 18. [I have adopted the modernized text in David Lyle Jeffrey's anthology, *A Burning and Shining Light* (Grand Rapids, Michigan: Eerdmans, 1987).]

[38]Andrew A. Bonar, ed., *The Works of Rev. Robert Murray McCheyne* (n.p.:Robert Carter & Brothers, 1883), 162–165.

[39]Phoebe Palmer, *Faith and Its Effects: Or Fragments from My Portfolio,*27th ed.(New York: Foster and Palmer, Jr., n.d.), 64–72.

[40]Al Bryant, compl., *Near the Sun: A Sourcebook of Daily Meditations from Charles Haddon Spurgeon* (Waco, Texas: Word Books, 1980), 9–10, 61.

[41]George Matheson, *My Aspirations,* (n.p.:Cassell, Petter, Galpin & Co., 1833), 29–31, 95–97.

[42]Hanna Whitall Smith, *The Christian's Secret of a Happy Life* (n.p.: The Christian Witness, 1885), 31–37.

[43]Andrew Murray, *With Christ in the School of Prayer* (Fleming H. Revell, n.d.), 180–182, 172–174. (I have taken the liberty to create some short paragraphs in the interest of readability.)

[44]Oswald Chambers, *My Utmost for His Highest* (n.p.: Simpkin Marshall, 1942), pp. 295, 314.

[45]Thomas R. Kelly, *A Testament of Devotion* (New York: Harper & Row, 1941), 112, 114, 116, 31–32, 35–36.

[46]William Temple, *Readings in St. John's Gospel* (New York: MacMillan, 1955), 226–228.

[47]Dietrich Bonhoeffer, *Life Together* (New York: Harper, 1954), pp. 26–30.

[48]Watchman Nee, *The Normal Christian Life* (Fort Washington, Penn,.: Christian Literature Crusade, 1961), 35-37.

[49]John Baillie, *A Diary of Private Prayer* (New York: Charles Scribner's Sons, 1949), 27, 65.

[50]Frank Cumbers, ed., *Daily Readings from W. E. Sangster* (Old Tappan, New Jersey: Revell, 1966), 55, 85.

[51]C. S. Lewis, *The Screwtape Letters* (London: Collins, 1942), 44–47.

[52]A. W. Tozer, *The Pursuit of God* (Camp Hill, Penn., Horizon House Edition), 62–71.

Acknowledgments

Grateful acknowledgment is made to the following for permission to use copyright material:

Baker Book House
> Excerpts from "On the Christian Life" by John Calvin, originally chapter 17 of the 1539 edition of the *Institutes,* the English translation found in Ford Lewis Battle's *The Piety of John Calvin,* © 1978.

Christian Publications
> Excerpts from *The Pursuit of God* by A. W. Tozer (Horizon House Edition).

Wm Collins Sons & Co. Ltd.
> Excerpts from *The Screwtape Letters* by C. S. Lewis, © 1942.

Dodd, Mead & Co.
> Excerpts from *My Utmost for His Highest* by Oswald Chambers.

Doubleday & Company
> Excerpts from *The Little Flowers of St. Francis of Assisi* by Raphael Brown, © 1958 Beverly H. Brown. Reprinted by permission of Doubleday & Company.

Harper & Brothers
> Excerpts from *Christian Perfection* by François Fenelon, © 1947.
> Excerpts from *Life Together* by Dietrich Bonhoeffer, © 1954.
> Excerpts from *A Testament of Devotion* by Thomas R. Kelly, © 1941.

ICS Publicatons
> Excerpts from *The Collected Works of St. Teresa of Avila,* © 1980.

Kingsway Publications
> Excerpt from *The Normal Christian Life* by Watchman Nee.

Macmillan Publishing Co.
> Excerpts from *A Diary of Private Prayer* by John Baillie, © 1949, 1977.
> Excerpts from *Readings in St. John's Gospel* by William Temple, © 1955.

Multnomah Press
> Excerpts from *The Love of God* by Bernard of Clairvaux, abridged and edited by James M. Houston, © 1983.

Thomas Nelson Publishers
> Excerpts from *The Practice of the Presence of God* by Brother Lawrence, © 1981.
> Excerpts from *Meditation on the Suffering of Christ* by Philipp Jakob Spener, found in *Pietists' Selected Writings,* The Classics of Western Spirituality, edited by Peter C. Erb, © 1983.

Paulist Press
> Excerpts from *Theologica Germanica,* Chapter 11. This translation is by Bengt Hoffman in *The Theologica Germanica of Martin Luther,* © 1980.
> Excerpts from *True Christianity* by Johann Arndt, translated by Peter C. Erb, © 1979.

Charles Scribner's Sons
> Excercpts from *A Diary of Private Prayer,* © renewed 1977 Jan Fowler Baillie. Reprinted with permission of Charles Scribner's Sons, an imprint of Macmillan Publishing Co.